Morris L. Venden

How Jesus
Treated People

Loud!

Pacific Press® Publishing Association
Nampa, Idaho
Oshawa, Ontario, Canada

Edited by Ken McFarland
Cover design by Michelle C. Petz
Cover illustration by Duane Tank and Nary Cruz

Library of Congress Cataloging-in-Publication Data

Venden, Morris L.
    How Jesus treated people
        1. Jesus Christ—Friends and associates.
2. Jesus Christ—Person and offices   I. Title.
BT303.V44   1985   232.9'5   85-16948

    ISBN 13: 978-0-8163-0621-3
    ISBN 10: 0-8163-0621-4

    06 07 08 09 • 13 12 11 10

Contents

Introduction

Jesus. You've heard about Him before, read about Him, sung about Him. You have pondered the contradictions of His life—how He is at once the Lamb of God and the Lion of the tribe of Judah. Both Advocate and Judge. Both Man and God. His teachings are the most simple and yet the most profound of all time.

Tiny children reached out to Him, unafraid. Yet when He came to earth, the empires of the world and of the kingdom of darkness trembled and were overcome. The guilty sinner finds acceptance and peace in His presence, while the self-righteous are strangely uncomfortable. He came to this earth the first time in poverty and reproach, but He will come again in power and glory indescribable, to reign as King of kings forever and ever.

No book can begin to paint a complete picture of Him. All the books ever written cannot describe Him fully, for the possibility for new insights into His life and character are as limitless as eternity itself.

This book offers simply another view of Jesus, a view with one particular emphasis in mind—how He treated people. It starts near the beginning of His adult ministry, where the gospel writers begin to give detailed descriptions of His interaction with various people or groups of people.

Again in this setting we see the paradox of His life. The common people heard Him gladly, but the priests and rulers—though they believed and trembled—rejected Him in the end. He welcomed the sinners, the harlots, the thieves. He treated the minority groups of His day with dignity. He had compassion on the fearful and timid and sorrowing, yet He rebuked the proud and self-sufficient.

And the result of His mission of salvation was that no one whose life He touched stayed the same. Either they accepted Him or rejected Him, when they saw who He was.

Put yourself in the picture as you follow these scenes from the life of Jesus. See Him reaching out to you, today, and allow Him to break down the barriers in your life. Jesus loves people—all kinds of people—and He has a place in His heart for you. May you come to know and trust Him better as you consider how Jesus treated people.

Introduction

How Jesus Treated the Money-Changers

After Jesus had been anointed the Messiah at the river Jordan, He attended the wedding at Cana, with the first of His disciples. The wedding was a family affair, for those involved were relatives of Jesus. There Jesus performed His first miracle by turning water into wine in answer to the faith of His mother, who had presented to Him the need of the occasion.

Immediately afterward, He traveled to Jerusalem for His first public act—the cleansing of the temple—which called tremendous attention to His mission.

Recorded in John 2, this episode provides interesting insights into how Jesus treated people. Please notice that the chapter begins with the wedding at Cana, followed by the cleansing of the temple, and then the interview with Nicodemus in John 3. The sequence is very interesting.

"After this [that is, after the wedding at Cana] he went down to Capernaum, he, and his mother, and his brethren, and his disciples: and they continued there not many days. And the Jews' passover was at hand, and Jesus went up to Jerusalem." John 2:12, 13.

On the way to Jerusalem, Jesus traveled among a large throng of people. But He was so little known at this point that He could mingle with the people going to Jerusalem as simply another person in the crowd. Before long that would be impossible. But now you see Jesus going from Capernaum to Jerusalem for the Passover as just a fellow traveler, talking to people who were talking about the Messiah to come.

"And [Jesus] found in the temple those that sold oxen and

sheep and doves, and the changers of money sitting: and when he had made a scourge of small cords, he drove them all out of the temple, and the sheep, and the oxen; and poured out the changers' money, and overthrew the tables; and said unto them that sold doves, Take these things hence; make not my Father's house an house of merchandise. And his disciples remembered that it was written, The zeal of thine house hath eaten me up." John 2:14-17.

What is a marketplace? A marketplace is where you buy and sell. A marketplace is where you get things that you have worked for. A marketplace is where you get what you earn, and you've earned what you get. A marketplace is the wrong place for a church, for a church is always to be a gift shop. Jesus wants His church to be a gift shop—not the kind of place where you *buy* gifts, but where you *receive* gifts. He doesn't want it to be a marketplace.

So this is why Jesus, on the very first day of His public ministry, did something so shocking that—before the day was over—some people already wanted to kill Him.

As we consider what He did that day, let's notice the groups of people to whom He spoke. There were merchants, who sold sheep and cattle and doves. There were money-changers, who helped people buy and sell by exchanging currency. And there were religious leaders, who served God for personal gain.

In the days of Jesus, the office of high priest sold for a million dollars. That was certainly not what God intended. With the office selling for a million dollars, often the one who bought it had himself in hock up to his ears and had to recoup his resources. So he would come to an agreement with the money-changers and the buyers and sellers. He would get a certain percentage on their business and pay back the loan he had taken out to become high priest. These things went on in the days of Jesus, religion had become so corrupt.

Then there were the disciples. Jesus treated them to a real shock. Up to this point they had apparently seen a rather subdued, low-profile picture of Jesus. They could almost have joined the boys and girls who sing, "Gentle Jesus, meek and mild, look upon this little child." But that day, they trembled.

Don't tell me that Jesus was white and emaciated, as the artists often paint Him. Anyone who had worked in the carpenter shop without power tools, cutting four-by-fours and all the rest of it by hand, didn't look at all like the weak person He is shown to be in many pictures. As He raised the scourge of cords, the sleeve must have fallen back from a muscular arm.

But that isn't what impressed the people most. Something else was at work that day. Divinity was flashing through. When the noise and confusion suddenly fell off to a deathly stillness as the eyes of one Man moved over the crowd, bigger forces were obviously at work. The disciples were surprised when they saw it happen.

However, we must remember that Jesus was not in the business of shouting in anger. There were tears in His voice when He uttered His scathing rebukes.

Another group in the temple that day was the teeming throng—the victims of the merit-mongers and those who served God for personal gain. At first glance, it might appear that Jesus cleansed the temple primarily to get the thieves out. But the truth is that He cleansed the temple to get the poor and the sick and the halt and the blind and the discouraged *in*. The cleansing of the temple was for the sake of the teeming throng.

They had been sold a bill of goods. They were people who had gotten the idea that you work your way to heaven—the idea that you *buy* sheep and you *buy* doves, when the Sheep is free and so is the Dove.

In the teeming throng were poor people who couldn't buy a sheep. And they would end up lying awake at night, staring at the ceiling, wondering if they would ever make it to the eternal kingdom. If religion were a thing that money could buy, the rich would live, and the poor would die.

Then there were the capable people who had the resources— the rich who could produce everything necessary to get good marks at the temple. They slept well at night because they had security. But it was a false security based on what they did themselves to earn God's favor. And somehow, sooner or later, God had to wake them up to this great deception.

Jesus wanted to reeducate the people who came to Jerusalem

just for the feast and then left. He wanted to reach those with no security and those with false security. So He drove out the thieves.

According to Matthew, He said, Don't make my Father's house a marketplace; don't make it a den of thieves. See Matthew 21:13. People were not only stealing money, they were stealing glory from God, peace from the people, and security from the incapable. Jesus drove them out.

But notice that the crowds of people pressed in instead of running out with the money-changers and the priests and the rabbis. And the confusion of the marketplace was replaced by sounds of praise and adoration from the sick who had been healed. Boys and girls, well now, joined in shouting His praises.

Even today people can shout and make fools of themselves at a football game or at the stadium, and everyone considers it normal. But if someone says Amen in church, he's considered weird. So when the rulers and money-changers who had fled the temple finally slowed down, gathered their courage, and drifted back toward the temple, they heard the sound of praise instead of the sound of a marketplace. And they were disturbed. They were far more comfortable with the sound of a marketplace than with the sound of praises to God.

But the good news is that Jesus didn't hate the thieves. Jesus was not out to get them. He loved the merchants, and He loved the money-changers. He loved the religious leaders. He would later go to feasts with them. He would attend gatherings of tax collectors. He would rub shoulders with priests and rulers. Jesus pitied them all for their fear and their ignorance. He longed to reach them with His love, as well as to minister to the teeming throng.

One thing happened that day not usually included in this story. In the crowd—perhaps behind one of the pillars, standing off to the side in the shadows—was a man. A lone man. He was one of the religious leaders—a member of the Sanhedrin. He stood and watched, and he was impressed.

Nicodemus saw the merchants go; he saw the money-changers go. He saw the tables toppled. He felt the inexplicable power emanating from the person of Jesus. He saw the tears; he heard the voice that broke and choked. He heard the cries of Hosanna. He saw the healing of the sick. He watched it all from the shadows. Apparently he didn't run with the rest. He watched.

And he said to himself, I must seek an interview with this Man. There's something here unaccounted for by human reasoning. So in John 3 you see Nicodemus coming to Jesus, directly as a result of His cleansing of the temple. Nicodemus came for himself to hear about the gift of salvation.

But now we come to an enigma—a problem. Jesus wants the temple to be a gift shop. He doesn't want it to be a marketplace. But the last book of the Bible speaks of *buying* gold tried in the fire and white raiment and eyesalve. Jesus Himself, in other parables, says we should buy because we've sold everything to get the pearl; we should sell everything to obtain the treasure hid in the field. What is He talking about?

Well, one thing we know He's *not* talking about is gold and silver. Gold is nothing in heaven. That's what they pave their streets with! The currency of heaven is selling all that *we* are or think we are—all that *we* have or think we have. It is realizing our own nothingness and being willing to get rid of our self-dependence. It is coming to Jesus and accepting His gifts. That's how the currency works.

When Jesus tells us to sell all and buy the field, what He is really saying is, Give up on yourself—give up on the thought that you can ever earn it. If you are a mighty man, He says, get rid of trusting in that. If you are rich, don't trust your riches. If you are smart or talented or good-looking, don't trust in those advantages. By admitting our helplessness to produce righteousness and by turning ourselves completely over to His control, we spend heaven's currency.

Trusting in God is probably one of the best definitions we could find for the oft-used Christian word, *surrender*. Trust involves depending upon another instead of yourself. But surrender isn't always easy. Sometimes we try so hard to give up on ourselves that we become more like ourselves. We forget that only Jesus can accomplish this work. It's a gift.

Faith is a gift. Love is a gift. White raiment is a gift. Repentance is a gift. Obedience is a gift. Victory is a gift. The Dove, or the Holy Spirit, is a gift—which brings all other blessings in His train. The Lamb is a gift—the Lamb of God who takes away the sins of the world. And surrender is a gift.

There's something else we should notice in this story. When we speak of the Holy Spirit, when we talk of the work God is doing in our hearts, we are reminded of a great truth taught by the cleansing of the temple. Jesus was announcing there His mission as the Messiah and entering upon His work, not only to save people forever, but to fulfill the purpose that every created being should be a temple for the indwelling of the Creator.

Because of sin, humanity had ceased to be a temple for God. Darkened and defiled by evil, the heart of man no longer revealed the glory of the Divine One. The courts of the temple in Jerusalem, filled with unholy traffic, represented all too truly the temple of the heart, defiled by the presence of sensual passions and unholy thoughts. In cleansing the temple from the world's buyers and sellers, Jesus announced His mission to cleanse the heart from the defilement of sin, from the earthly desires, the selfish lusts, the evil habits that corrupt the soul.

Have you discovered yet that no one can of himself cast out the evil throng that has taken possession of the heart? Have you discovered yet that only Christ can cleanse the soul temple? But He will not force an entrance. He does not come into the heart as He did into the temple of old. Instead, He says, "Behold, I stand at the door, and knock." Revelation 3:20.

He invites you to accept Him not only as the Lamb of God, but as the High Priest in the heavens who can be touched with the feelings of our infirmities and was in all points tempted like as we are. He invites you to come boldly before the throne of grace, that you may obtain mercy and find grace to help in time of need. See Hebrews 4:15, 16. All power in heaven and earth resides in the person of Jesus Christ. Without Him, no one can hope to succeed, but with Him, failure is impossible.

> All hail the power of Jesus' name!
> Let angels prostrate fall.
> —Edward Perronet

How Jesus Treated the Fallen

In the little village of Bethany, about three miles from Jerusalem, lived two sisters, Mary and Martha, and their brother Lazarus. Apparently Lazarus was the breadwinner of the family. Father and mother were gone, so Mary, Martha, and Lazarus lived together in this little village.

You can see Lazarus going to work every day with his lunch pail, coming home tired, perhaps catching up on the evening news, and going to bed—only to begin all over again the next day.

Martha was the Martha-type! She could run a potluck, a wedding dinner, or a church picnic. She was never happier than when out in the kitchen, trying a new recipe. Martha was a good person. She never did anything wrong. Probably the worst thing she ever did was to chew her fingernails when the Mix-Master didn't work. She was religious. It was pretty hard not to be at that time and in that locality. Every Sabbath morning she went down the beaten path from her house to the synagogue.

Mary, on the other hand, was more interested in the social scene. She loved people. Whenever there was a church social or picnic, Mary was always asked to greet the people and help them feel at home. She was attractive—perhaps stunning.

But Mary carried a secret load of guilt and misery that no one suspected. It had to do with her Uncle Simon. Simon the Pharisee.

Now Pharisees got good marks in those days. They don't today, but they did back then. If anyone was asked what his son was doing, he was never happier than to say, "My son is a Pharisee."

So Simon got good marks in Bethany. He was a church leader. He was respected in the community. People even respected him for his close association with the family of Mary, Martha, and Lazarus. As their closest of kin, he was expected to look out for his relatives. But one day Simon began to look too long at Mary, and being in the position he was, he soon led Mary to give in to his demands.

Apparently no one knew what was happening. Simon continued to lead out at the synagogue. Mary continued to smile and chat and charm. But the load of guilt she carried was almost overwhelming.

A few times she tried to reason with her uncle—tried to break from his control. But women weren't listened to much in those days, and it was her word against his. He threatened her with public exposure and even death. He blamed her for the problem in the first place. And Mary finally gave up hope of ever being free again.

As so often happens when a religious person becomes involved in secret sin, Mary began trying to punish herself. She was constantly reminded by the lambs and the blood, by the morning and evening sacrifices, that someone had to pay. And if you are trying to pay for your own sin and trying to punish yourself, one of the best methods is to commit the same sin again. This will make you feel even worse. And making yourself feel worse is a convenient form of self-punishment.

If self-punishment continues, you commit the same sin again and again and again, until finally there's only one thing left to do—to jump off a bridge somewhere as the final form of self-punishment.

So Mary began trying to punish herself, and as a result she came to be known around town as a loose woman. Mothers would talk over the back fence. "Have you heard about Mary?"

"Yes."

"Watch out for Mary. Keep your young people away from Mary."

The talk continued to spread until one day things got so bad for Mary in Bethany that she decided to leave. She packed her belongings and traveled down the road from the mountain with seven hills until she came to a little village near the sea, called Magdala. She was later to become known as Mary from Magdala, or Mary Magdalene.

I see her going into Magdala determined to start a new life. She looks for work. She tries the local dry-goods store. But they don't need her there. She tries the Stop-&-Shop, but they have all the help they need. Perhaps she even tries the catering service of Magdala, hoping to get by on the few things she's picked up from Martha. But they don't need any help.

After walking the streets of Magdala, looking for work and getting hungry, one day Mary gives in to the temptation to earn some easy money. "Why not? You're already into it. There are more lambs where the others came from."

Mary was able to find those willing to pay her price. And strangely enough, she found a degree of acceptance. But her load of guilt became heavier and heavier. She found it harder and harder to forget the happier days in Bethany, before the death of her parents, before Simon—the days when she had known peace.

One day a traveling Preacher came to the village of Magdala. He didn't go to the synagogue to speak. There wouldn't have been room to hold the crowds. He talked to the people right out there in the open air. He said things like, "Come unto me, all ye that labour and are heavy laden, and I will give you rest." Matthew 11:28. "Whoever comes to me, I will in no wise cast out." See John 6:37. "I am not come to call the righteous, but sinners to repentance." Matthew 9:13.

Mary lingered at the edge of the crowd, listening. She had never heard things like this before. As she listened, her heart was strangely warmed. She waited until the crowds left, and then she went to Him and poured out her great need for help.

This traveling Preacher went to His knees and prayed for her to His Father, that she might have the help she needed. Mary accepted a new Master. The devil was rebuked. And Mary was converted right there.

What a beautiful story!

I would like to be able to say that the story ended there and that Mary lived happily ever after. But that's not quite the way it was. Because the Preacher left town, and Mary didn't. Perhaps she should have. There in Magdala were the same people, the same friends, the same voices in the marketplace who would call her name. As the days went by, Mary discovered that even though she had accepted the peace this Preacher had to offer, the downward pull was still strong. And Mary fell.

In this story we have one of the most beautiful examples in all the Bible of how Jesus treated the fallen.

Jesus came to town again. Again the crowds gathered around Him, listening. And again Mary found her way to the edge of the crowd, wondering—wondering if it could still be true. Yes. He was still saying, "Whoever comes to me, I will in no wise cast out." It was still good.

She went to Him and discovered that He still accepted her. Again she poured out her need with tears. And again He went to His knees and cried to His Father in her behalf. And again Jesus left town, and Mary didn't.

I'd like to say that was the end of the story. But Mary fell again and again and again. But whenever Jesus came to town, Mary was in the crowd. She was always drawn to the One who said, "Whoever comes to me, I will in no wise cast out."

Then one day Mary received an invitation to go to Jerusalem. Perhaps the messengers offered a large sum of money for her services. Perhaps they offered arrangements for a marriage. Or possibly they told her she was needed at home—that her Uncle Simon had sent for her. Whatever the method, Mary was framed. And the public exposure she had feared so long became a reality.

The door to the apartment that had been provided burst open. Loud voices denounced her as a sinner, deserving to die. Hard hands grasped her and dragged her out into the street. Mary closed her eyes and wished that she could die.

She was forced through the crowds and thrown down in the presence of Jesus. Shouts of accusation filled the air as Mary huddled there, trembling, waiting for the final blows to fall. Surely she had filled up her cup of guilt—even Jesus wouldn't be able to help her now.

As she waited there in her fear and shame, the sounds of the mob grew quiet. Mary braced herself for the first stone. But instead she heard a gentle voice asking, "Where are your accusers? Has no man condemned you?"

Mary raised her head. Her accusers had all disappeared. Unbelievingly she heard the words of Jesus, "Neither do I condemn you. Go, and sin no more." Once again Mary knelt at the feet of Jesus, crying out for His forgiveness, for His power. See John 8. And that day Mary learned something she hadn't learned before—and that we're way overdue to learn today.

She learned that it was possible to find Jesus through His Word—to pray to Him wherever she was. She learned that it was possible to stay at the feet of Jesus even when He wasn't in town. Have you discovered that yet? It's hard to sin when you are sitting at Jesus' feet. There is power there.

And even though Jesus went on His way, Mary was ready to continue to be at His feet, seeking Him and His presence.

And then Mary got a bright idea. Why not go back home to Bethany to Martha and Lazarus? No sooner did the idea surface than the very blood began to sing in her veins. Surely the power of Jesus would be sufficient even for dealing with her Uncle Simon. So she packed up her things and headed for Bethany.

As she came within sight of the town, she began to hear a lonely cry common in those days. The closer she got, the clearer it sounded. It was a leper on the outside of the village walls of Bethany.

The sound was common enough, all right. In those days, leprosy was called the stroke—the finger of God. Leprosy was considered a judgment—in fact, any sickness was considered a judgment on account of sin. But leprosy was the worst. It made no difference whether you were the mayor of the city, a leader in the synagogue, or a Pharisee. When you got leprosy, you were pronounced unclean. You were pushed out of town. You sat by the side of the road, publishing your calamity by crying, "Unclean, unclean," begging for someone to throw you a morsel of bread.

So as Mary came near, she hardly noticed the cry, until suddenly she recognized something in the voice crying, "Unclean." It was Simon, her uncle who had led her into sin.

And when *I* heard that, I said to myself, "Good! Good for Simon! Let him rot by the side of the road!" That tells you something about *my* thinking.

Mary pulled her shawl across her face and went on to the village of Bethany, trying to take in the fact that she had nothing more to fear from Simon the Pharisee.

She was so eager to see Martha and Lazarus again. She rushed up the steps, through the door. A joyful reunion followed, and tears flowed as once again the family was united.

But word began to get around. "Mary's back. Watch out for Mary." "Did you hear what happened in Jerusalem?"

"They say she's changed."

"Well, she won't be changed for long. I've heard she changed before, and it never lasted." "You watch her." That's the way people talked in those days.

It was hard for Mary as they whispered and gossiped, but she stayed, determined to share with someone else the news about the Friend she had found, the Friend who always loved and accepted her, the Friend who did not condemn her, but who gave her power to sin no more. She wanted others to find the Friend at whose feet she loved to sit. And she looked forward to the time when He would visit the town of Bethany.

Sure enough, He did. One day Jesus traveled up the hills to Bethany with His twelve companions. As He came into town, He too heard the cry Mary had heard—"Unclean, unclean!"

It seems almost impossible to understand. But Jesus found it hard to go past lepers. He couldn't seem to pass them by, even when nine tenths of them never bothered to say Thank You.

So Jesus stopped at the cry of Simon the leper. He touched the untouchable and made him well again—just like that. He didn't insist that Simon first accept Him as Saviour. He just cleansed him.

I used to think that the only people ever healed were those about ready for translation. But Jesus healed Simon—the sinner, the impure, the unrepentant—when he hadn't even accepted Jesus as Saviour. Jesus made Simon whole because of who Jesus was, not because of who Simon was. Have you ever wondered how Mary might have felt when she heard the news? Perhaps Jesus reassured her that Simon's power over her was still broken.

But healing is a heavy one to lay on a Pharisee. A Pharisee is used to *earning* his rewards. This gift from Jesus was too much for Simon to take. So after he had gone back to Bethany and been reinstated in his position in the village, you see him tossing and turning by night, pacing the floors by day, trying to figure out what to do. He hadn't been able to earn or merit being healed. But suddenly he got an idea. He hadn't earned it beforehand, but why not earn it afterward? Simon said to himself, I'll pay this Man back for what He's done. I will throw a feast in His honor." See Matthew 26; John 12.

Now his mind was going fast. Martha would be the one to do the catering—that would be all right. But Mary wasn't invited. Simon was uncomfortable around Mary. Who knows? The leprosy may have come upon him because of his involvement in her direction—better not take chances.

When the night of the banquet came, Mary sat at home. She would have enjoyed the crowds and people, even though some of them were still cool when she came around. But what really disappointed Mary was the fact that she couldn't see Jesus.

She had heard Jesus say, not long before, that He was going to Jerusalem and that there He would be betrayed into the hands of sinners. They were going to put Him to death. At great personal expense, Mary had purchased an alabaster box of ointment to anoint Jesus after His death. But Mary doesn't like the idea of giving flowers at a funeral. She wishes to give her gift of love to Jesus now.

Suddenly she grabs her box of ointment and hurries down the quiet streets of Bethany, planning as she goes. She rushes through the back door and on through the kitchen. Martha tries to stop her, but nothing stops Mary.

She moves quietly across the darkened room, lighted with those little olive-oil lamps, to the place where Jesus is sitting. Her plan is to open the box of ointment, anoint Jesus' feet, and leave. And no one will ever know.

But she's forgotten something. When you open an alabaster box of the most costly ointment, it *screams*.

Now every eye is turned her way. There's Simon at the head of the table, looking daggers at her. There's Judas and all the others. She fumbles with the ointment. It spills. She has forgotten to bring a towel or anything to wipe it up, so Mary does what in those days was unforgivable—only a woman of the streets would let down her hair. But she doesn't think of that. She lets down her hair and begins to wipe up the ointment with her hair.

And Simon, at the end of the table, thinks to himself, "If this Man was really a prophet, He would know what kind of woman this is."

About that time, Mary hears the friendly words of Jesus, "Let her alone. She has done a good thing. And wherever the gospel is preached, this story about Mary will be told."

Then Jesus turned to Simon and said, "Simon."

And right there Simon got sweaty palms. Jesus said, "Simon, I have something to say to you." Simon braced himself, expecting the mask to be torn from his face. He'd heard about this Jesus who could read people's thoughts, and he prepared for the worst.

But Jesus tells a little story about two debtors, one of whom owed a large debt and one who only owed a little. Both the debtors were freely forgiven. See Luke 7. Nobody understood the story, except for Simon and Mary and Jesus. But Simon got the message. Did he ever get the message!

Simon was overwhelmed by the love and compassion of a Man who could have exposed him for what he really was, but who instead veiled His message in a parable and protected him from his friends.

Simon's heart was broken. He realized all that Jesus had done for him and that he could never repay it. And right there, at his own feast, Simon accepted Jesus as Master and Saviour and Lord. Jesus got Simon too! What a story!

And if Jesus could accept Mary and Simon, surely He ought to be able to accept you and me today and to forgive us and love us to the end.

How Jesus Treated the Fearful

Have you ever been afraid? When you were small, were you ever afraid when the lightning flashed and the thunder rolled? Have you ever been afraid when you were alone at night? Have you ever been afraid of growing old, of having to have surgery, or of losing your job? Have you ever been afraid of change, of making new friends, of losing the old? Have you ever been afraid of not making it to heaven, of losing out on eternal life?

Fear is as old as sin. The first thing we notice in Genesis, after Adam and Eve ate the fruit, is that they hid themselves. God came looking for them and said, "Adam, where are you? Why did you hide?"

And he said, "I was afraid."

Why was he afraid? Because of sin.

The last book of the Bible, the book of Revelation, gives fear very poor marks. "He that overcometh shall inherit all things; and I will be his God, and he shall be my son. But the *fearful*, and unbelieving, and the abominable, and murderers, and whoremongers, and sorcerers, and idolaters, and all liars, shall have their part in the lake which burneth with fire and brimstone." Revelation 21:7, 8, emphasis supplied. What a motley bunch of bedfellows fear shows up with. Fear gets bad marks in Scripture, because God has something better than fear for His people.

Now there's an interesting episode in the life of Jesus that takes us right into this subject. It's found in Mark 4—the story of the storm on the Sea of Galilee. "In the same day, when even was come, he saith unto them, Let us pass over unto the other side." Mark 4:35.

Notice that it was Jesus' suggestion to cross the lake that evening. It wasn't the disciples' idea—their folly. It wasn't a matter of their getting themselves into a tight place. They set out to cross the lake at the command and invitation of Jesus Himself.

Jesus said, Let's go over to the other side. "And when they had sent away the multitude, they took him even as he was in the ship. And there were also with him other little ships. And there arose a great storm of wind, and the waves beat into the ship, so that it was now full. And he was in the hinder part of the ship, asleep on a pillow: and they awake him, and say unto him, Master, carest thou not that we perish?

"And he arose, and rebuked the wind, and said unto the sea, Peace, be still. And the wind ceased, and there was a great calm. And he said unto them, Why are ye so fearful? how is it that ye have no faith? And they feared exceedingly, and said one to another, What manner of man is this, that even the wind and the sea obey him?" Mark 4:36-41. You would be awed, too, by such an experience. But let's go back and try to put ourselves into the picture and imagine what it was like that day.

The day had been a busy one. Jesus had told many parables. He had healed the sick. He had brought comfort to troubled hearts. Now He was tired. He was overcome with hunger and exhaustion. God? Yes. Hungry and tired—maybe even more tired than the rest of them! So they set out across the sea to a quiet place to find some rest.

Suddenly, as so often happened on that sea, the wind whipped down from the slopes of Gadara and churned the water into a frothy frenzy. The waves were lashed into fury by the howling winds and dashed fiercely over the disciples' boat, threatening to engulf it. Helpless in the grasp of the tempest, their hope failed as they saw the boat beginning to fill.

Absorbed in their efforts to save themselves, they had forgotten that Jesus was on board. Now, seeing their labor vain and only death before them, they remembered at whose command they had set out to cross the sea. In Jesus was their only hope.

In their helplessness and despair they cried, "Master! Master!"
The account of this episode as recorded in Matthew uses the
words, "Lord, *save* us." Matthew 8:25. They didn't say, "Lord,
help us." There's a big difference between the two. This really
speaks to the question of divine power and human effort, if you
please. Where was their cooperation? It was in coming to the
end of their own resources and realizing that all they could do
was to cry out, "Lord, save us." He was going to have to do it *all*.

They had already done everything they could do. They were
hardy fishermen who had lived all their lives on the shores of
this lake. They knew Galilee. They knew the hills and the
winds and the storms. They knew about big waves and how to
keep their boat under control. They understood how to distrib-
ute their weight and how to pull on the oars. This really wasn't
Jesus' department. He had been a carpenter, not a fisherman.
He was a preacher now, and His job was to talk to the crowds
and heal the sick. He had done His work all day and was now
sleeping. Now was the time for them to handle things themselves. This was their area of expertise.

But finally they discovered that they were not able to handle
the storm. They had tried everything they knew, to no avail.
Their boat was sinking. At last they turned to Him with the
cry, "Lord, save us: we perish!"

Never did a soul utter that cry unheeded. Jesus arose. He
lifted His hands, so often employed in deeds of mercy, and said
to the angry sea, "Peace, be still." Mark 4:39. The storm ceases.
The billows sink to rest. The clouds roll away. The stars shine
forth. The boat rests on a quiet sea. Then, turning to His disciples, Jesus asked sorrowfully, "Why are ye so fearful? how is it
that ye have no faith?" Verse 40.

Well, what would you do under those circumstances if you
did have faith? When you have faith and you're out on the free-
way, headed on a beeline course straight for a head-on collision,
what do you do? Relax and smile? Let go of the steering wheel?
Look out the side window at the passing scenery?

Perhaps we could remember the Moravian missionaries who
were on board ship with John Wesley. He had gone to America
to convert the Indians and had ended up frustrated, saying, "I

came to America to convert the Indians, but who will convert John Wesley?"

Now a storm came up on the Atlantic, and it looked as if they were going to the bottom of the sea. But the Moravians were not afraid.

John Wesley was impressed. He asked them why they were so calm. They said, "Oh, we're not afraid to die."

Just because you have faith doesn't mean you won't go to the bottom of the sea. Faith doesn't mean you won't be burned at the stake with Huss and Jerome. Faith doesn't mean you will be cured of cancer. But people who have faith are not afraid to die.

And there's something else. People who have faith don't look at God as a last resort. In any unexpected trial, they turn to Him as naturally as the flower turns to the sun.

Two people were talking about a friend who was in very poor health. One told of the various cures and medicines and doctors that had been tried, without success. And he finally ended his description by saying, "I guess that all there is left to do is to pray."

To which his companion replied, "Alas! Has it come to *that*?"

The person who has faith never forgets that Jesus is on board, but turns to Him in every emergency.

Well, the disciples didn't have faith. Jesus reminded them of their lack, but He still saved them. And that's good news. He saved them in spite of their lack of faith.

We have many fears today. We have fears concerning our health and our children and our houses and lands. We are afraid of what others may think of us. The poor man fears for want, and the rich man fears for loss. We have fears about the church and about the future and about our own salvation.

Just having Jesus on board is not enough to keep us from having fears—it wasn't for the disciples. Even though Jesus was on board, they forgot Him when the storm came and the waves were high. And that is still possible today. We can have a relationship with Jesus and still not depend upon Him for all things. The disciples had a relationship with Jesus. They walked together, talked together, prayed together, worked together. They were very close to Jesus. But there were times when they demonstrated that in spite of their close relationship with Jesus, they still did not depend upon Him all the time.

But Jesus stayed with them. He was patient with them and encouraged them to trust in Him. And the time came when these same fearful disciples could fearlessly face boiling caldrons of oil, the sword, the flames, or crucifixion upside down; for they had learned the lessons of faith and trust Jesus had tried to teach them.

The love of Jesus drives out fear and makes the difference. The Bible says that perfect love casts out fear. See 1 John 4:18. At first glance, you might ask, Well, who has perfect love? If we don't have perfect love, how can we avoid fear? But it's not our perfect love. Christ is the only One who has perfect love. And it's His perfect love that casts out fear.

I suppose most parents have gone through the experience of tossing the little ones into the air when they were two or three years old. I used to love to toss them into the air and watch them laugh and smile in complete peace, because Daddy loved them, and he'd catch them.

One night we began a game on the piano bench. My son would climb up on the piano bench and jump off into my arms. This went on and on until I was exhausted. And I said, "That's it. No more."

"One more time, Daddy. One more time."

And finally, in an attempt to bring an end to the game, I walked away, figuring he would get the message.

But he never even looked. This time when he climbed up on the piano bench and took off into the air, I was on the other side of the room, and he had a bad fall. I felt terrible! But there's nothing like the love and trust of a little child.

Jesus is the One who said it: "Except ye be converted, and become as little children—" Matthew 18:3. And He invites us to cast all our care upon Him, for He cares for us. See 1 Peter 5:7. But there's one big difference. He never gets tired. He's always there. He has promised, "I will never leave you or forsake you." See Hebrews 13:5. But no one really casts himself totally upon Jesus until he realizes that love and also realizes that he has come to the end of his own resources.

Notice where Jesus was during the storm. He was asleep in the boat. He wasn't afraid. Well, we're tempted to think that it was because He was God. The songwriter says, This is God, and "no water can swallow the ship where lies, the Master of ocean, and earth, and skies."—M. A. Baker.

But something is here that we must not miss—something about how Jesus lived His life. When Jesus awakened to meet the storm, He was in perfect peace. There was no trace of fear in word or look, for no fear was in His heart. But He did not rest in the possession of Almighty power. It was not as "the Master of ocean, and earth, and skies" that He reposed in quiet. That power He had laid down. He had said, "I can of mine own self do nothing." John 5:30. He trusted in His Father's might. It was in faith—faith in God's love and care—that Jesus rested. And the power of that word which stilled the storm was the power of God from above Him rather than the power of God from within Him.

If the disciples had trusted in Him, they would have been kept in peace. Their fear in time of danger revealed their unbelief. In their efforts to save themselves, they forgot Jesus, and it was only when in the despair of self-dependence they turned to Him that He could save them.

Notice here the spiritual application involved in the calming of the storm. When it comes to salvation, how often we find ourselves worrying about whether or not we will be saved. And all of this turns our attention away from Jesus, our only source of strength. We are invited to commit the keeping of our souls to God and trust in Him. See 1 Peter 4:19. He will never leave us if we've accepted Him as our hope and our salvation. We can leave Him, but He will never leave us.

And what about living the Christian life? Some people can accept the sacrifice of Jesus at the cross, but when they read Revelation 3:5, "He that overcometh, the same shall be clothed in white raiment; and I will not blot out his name out of the book of life," they are ready to despair. They say, I can never do that. I can never be an overcomer. I fall and fail too often and too easily.

How often the disciples' experience is ours! When the tempests of temptation gather and the fierce lightnings flash and the waves sweep over us, we battle with the storm alone, forgetting that there is One who can help us. We trust to our own strength till our hope is lost and we are ready to perish. Then we remember Jesus, and if we call upon Him to save us, we shall not cry in vain. Though He sorrowfully reproves our unbelief and self-confidence, He never fails to give us the help we need.

There is only one thing to fear for the Christian—only one legitimate fear. We should fear to trust our own strength. We should fear to withdraw our hand from the hand of Christ or attempt to walk the Christian pathway alone.

But so long as we depend upon Christ, as *He* depended upon His Father here on this earth, we are secure. We have no need to fear as we trust His perfect love.

How Jesus Treated the Outcast

This is the story of a man who raised the roof and got let down by his friends! It is found in Mark 2:1 and onward. "And again [Jesus] entered into Capernaum after some days; and it was noised that he was in the house. And straightway many were gathered together, insomuch that there was no room to receive them, no, not so much as about the door: and he preached the word unto them.

"And they come unto him, bringing one sick of the palsy, which was borne of four. And when they could not come nigh unto him for the press, they uncovered the roof where he was: and when they had broken it up, they let down the bed wherein the sick of the palsy lay.

"When Jesus saw their faith, he said unto the sick of the palsy, Son, thy sins be forgiven thee. . . .

"That ye may know that the Son of man hath power on earth to forgive sins, (he saith to the sick of the palsy,) I say unto thee, Arise, and take up thy bed, and go thy way into thine house.

"And immediately he arose, took up the bed, and went forth before them all; insomuch that they were all amazed, and glorified God, saying, We never saw it on this fashion." Mark 2:1-12.

Who was this man who becomes the central character of this story? I'd like to suggest that he was a nobody about town. He was an invalid. He was a shut-in. He didn't make his mark in the town very often, that's for sure. He was, on top of that, an outcast. Anyone suffering or afflicted or diseased was charged with being a great sinner—a great sinning sinner! And in this case, the charge happened to be true.

At times Jesus said that the disease or the affliction had nothing to do with a person's sin. He had said that about the blind man in John 9. The disciples had asked, "Who sinned, this man or his parents?"

And Jesus said, "Neither."

Yet the blind man was considered a great sinner because he was blind. The man in this story was not only considered a great sinner, but he was one. The evidence is that his affliction was the result of a life of sin, and many Bible commentators consider that it was a social disease. So he was an outcast.

One by one his friends had faded away, except his sinning friends. I suppose we could even conjecture that the ones who carried him to Jesus were of the same ilk.

This man knew what it was like to have a burning conscience and to push it and sublimate it into the back chambers of his mind. He knew the evil of sin by experience, not just by observation. He knew what it was to be an outcast. He knew guilt and what the devil does in pounding a person with guilt. He knew the abhorrence of sin, in spite of still loving it. He knew the unrest, the unsatisfied desires, the bondage from which he struggled in vain to be free.

He knew that even his motives were not right. *Why* did he want to go to look for help? Have you ever discovered that some calamity or affliction or sorrow causes the devil to beat you over the head with your selfish motives for turning to God at that time? It's called the theology of despair—to be interested in God only when trouble comes.

So we see this man coming to Jesus. That's the one thing he did right. He had tried other methods, and he had been let down many times. He was about to be let down into a grave somewhere, for the disease had reached an advanced stage. He had tried the doctors, and they had let him down, pronouncing him incurable. He had tried the Pharisees and church leaders, and they had let him down. They had said he was hopeless, a great sinner, an outcast by God and man. His friends too had let him down. But on this last try, when they let him down through the roof, it turned out to be the greatest moment of his life.

A large crowd of people surrounded Jesus. Capernaum was no small village—not in those days. If you go there today, it's rather quiet except for tourists with flashing cameras. But you can see the ruins there on the shore of the Sea of Galilee. You can see the remnants of Peter's house, where this experience took place.

After Jesus had cleansed the temple, He had left Judea and come to Galilee to begin His ministry there. Already the demoniac had been set free, right in the synagogue. The word of that had raced around town, reaching even those who didn't go to church. And this man too had heard.

Peter's wife's mother had been healed, and later that same night after the sun had set, crowds of people had been healed before Jesus finally disappeared into the hills to pray.

Something else had happened, unheard of since the days of Elisha. A leper had been cleansed. As that report made the rounds, the crowds became so large that Jesus had to withdraw from Capernaum to a desert place in order to find relief.

Now Jesus was in Capernaum again, in Peter's house. It was so crowded there was no way to get inside. But at the man's own suggestion, his friends carried him to the roof, broke up the tiles, and let him down between the beams.

This would have been embarrassing to anyone carrying ordinary inhibitions. Can you imagine yourself doing that—putting yourself at the mercy of the jeering crowd? Everyone was staring at him as he came down in front of them all. But he was at the end of his own resources. When a person is at death's door, nothing else matters.

The people were there—the eager, the reverent, the unbelieving, the curious. The spy ring was there from Jerusalem—the Pharisees and Sadducees already out for Jesus' life. You can see the teeming throng, inside and outside of the house, listening through the windows and standing in the doorways. You can hear the sudden silence in the room after the pounding on the roof and feel the tension in the air as a lone man is let down into the very presence of Jesus.

The story says Jesus saw *their* faith. Don't miss the fact that the faith of the four who carried the man was also involved. We

don't know their names. We don't sing about them or tell the
stories of their lives. But they brought this man in the arms of
their faith into the presence of Jesus.

Now come the words that bring on the big moment of this
man's life. "My son." My son? You mean the God of the universe
calls someone like this His son? What about the God of justice
we've heard about? What about the God who has a list and is
checking it twice, trying to see how many people He can keep
out of heaven? *God* called this man, with his track record, "My
son"?

Yes, this is God talking. This is God saying, "My son."

Then Matthew adds a little phrase that Mark doesn't have in
his account of the story—"Be of good cheer." See Matthew 9:2. I
like that phrase. Is it possible today that anyone needs to cheer
up? Is it possible to be bogged down with guilt and remorse and
sin? Is there anyone today who can look at this story and see
more than just a history lesson, who can put himself in the picture?

Do we have those today who represent the teeming throng—
the curious, the eager, the reverent, the unbelieving? Do we
have those today who may represent the paralyzed man? If so,
then these words still apply—"Be of good cheer; thy sins be forgiven thee."

Jesus knew that at the top of this man's list was his desire to
have peace with God. Jesus also knew that this would bring all
other blessings in its train. So He said, "My son, thy sins be
forgiven."

This man was so concerned about peace with God, over anything else, that he was content to live or die—it made no difference—if he could just have his sins forgiven. The rest of it he
was happy to leave in God's hands.

I had a friend during college days, a quiet sort, a little older
than the rest of us. He was back from Korea where he had been
in the Marines. He had been in charge of a platoon of men. One
night, under cover of darkness, with only the stars above, they
had started up a mountain to take it for the Allies.

They had understood that the hill behind them had been
cleared, but someone had done a sloppy job of it, and a lone

Communist machine gunner was left on the hill.

As they started up the mountain, suddenly the machine gun opened fire on them. The gunner swept across the bottom row of his rank, then he raised the machine gun a couple of degrees and came back the other way. Then he raised it and came across again. He was very clever with his firing.

My friend, at the head of the platoon, knew he didn't have much time. He heard his men groaning and moaning and dying below him.

But he had grown up in a Christian home. He knew about Jesus and the second coming and heaven and forever. He had turned his back on all of it. But now, in spite of his wrong motives, he looked toward heaven and said, "God, I don't have much time. And I don't ask you to save my life. I don't deserve anything. But would you please help me to come up in the right resurrection?"

That's all he was interested in—peace with God. The rest of it could come or go.

But strangely enough, he came back from the hill unscathed. He came to college to study to be a minister, and ever since has been back in the armed forces as a chaplain, trying to help others like himself. Why did he do it? Because God had given him a bonus—not only forgiveness and peace and a hope of eternity, but life here and now. And when that happens to you, you've got to tell somebody!

So this paralyzed man settled back on his cot or his mattress or whatever it was, rejoicing in the good news, "My son, your sins are forgiven." A new glow came to his face. His eyes, even his body functions, began to change. It's hard to know at what point the forgiveness and the healing merge, but he's a new man. He lies there in complete bliss and happiness.

But there's always someone in the crowd to spoil it. The church leaders were thinking dark thoughts. And Jesus picked up on their thoughts and their body language. He said, "Whether is it easier to say to the sick of the palsy, Thy sins be forgiven thee; or to say, Arise, and take up thy bed, and walk? But that ye may know that the Son of man hath power on earth to forgive sins, (he saith to the sick of the palsy,) I say unto thee,

Arise, take up thy bed, and go thy way into thine house." Mark 2:9-11.

Was it easy for the palsied man to obey Jesus' words—or was it hard? When the Creator spoke, in the beginning, even the dust jumped to attention! At His command, worlds came into existence. Would it have been easy for the man to stay lying on his cot?

Sometimes we get bogged down in trying to decide what might have happened if the paralytic had not believed. What if he had stopped to analyze, to decide which came first, his faith or moving his muscles? There was no time for any of that! I would like to propose that when you are in the presence of the Life Giver and He says, Arise, take up your bed and walk, you do just that! You don't pause for dialogue or debate. You rise up immediately in the presence of the mighty creative word of God.

The man jumped to his feet. He took up his bed. And please notice—now he was somebody! He didn't have to go back through the roof! There was no room before, but the crowd suddenly found room now.

The man walked out the door, carrying his bed, and headed toward home, his face aglow with the wonder of the miracle. There is no evidence that his wife or children had come with him this day on this mission. They must have seen him leave home many times—for the doctors, the miracle workers, or the latest quacks. They must often have watched while he returned slowly in defeat. So they stayed home.

Now you see them looking out the window, between the shutters, or over the railing of the front porch. They can't believe it. It doesn't look like father, but it is father! He's running, jumping, almost prancing with excitement. He has new life. He has met the Saviour.

They gather around him, and he tells the story. The evidence is that wife and children from that moment on would gladly have given their lives for the Lord Jesus Christ.

Why did Jesus do it? Why did He come to people with healing? Because He wanted them all to know that He has power on earth to forgive sins. Jesus made sinners His best friends on earth, and He still has the same acceptance and forgiveness and power today.

A lot of people lack assurance and certainty and peace today. But I would like to invite you to join the poor paralyzed man, who proved that regardless of who you are or where you've been or what you've done, you are still accepted when you come to Jesus. You can still be forgiven.

This can cause you to walk with a new spring in your step, with new life in the soul, for God not only has power to forgive, but to heal and change and enable you to walk in newness of life as well. It all happens in the presence of Jesus.

How thankful we can be today that we can still come into the presence of Jesus, and that He's promised to accept us and forgive and cleanse.

The psalmist expressed it in these words:

Bless the Lord, O my soul:
   and all that is within me, bless his holy name.
Bless the Lord, O my soul,
   and forget not all his benefits:
     who forgiveth all thine iniquities;
     who healeth all thy diseases;
     who redeemeth thy life from destruction;
     who crowneth thee with lovingkindess and
      tender mercies.
                    —Psalm 103:1-4

How Jesus Treated the Brokenhearted

Have you ever been to a good funeral? Do you think it is possible to describe a funeral as "good"? Keep the possibility in mind as we look at the three accounts in Scripture where Jesus faced what we call death. We will consider them to discover how Jesus treated the brokenhearted.

The first of these accounts is found in Luke 7, beginning with verse 11: "And it came to pass the day after, that he went into a city called Nain; and many of his disciples went with him, and much people. Now when he came nigh to the gate of the city, behold, there was a dead man carried out, the only son of his mother, and she was a widow: and much people of the city was with her. And when the Lord saw her, he had compassion on her, and said unto her, Weep not. And he came and touched the bier: and they that bare him stood still. And he said, Young man, I say unto thee, Arise. And he that was dead sat up, and began to speak. And he delivered him to his mother. And there came a fear on all: and they glorified God, saying, That a great prophet is risen up among us; and That God hath visited his people." Verses 11-16.

Wasn't that a good funeral? I like that one! It didn't start out very well, but it ended in a triumphal entry back into the village of Nain.

Let's try to piece together the story just a little. The village of Nain was about twenty to twenty-five miles from Capernaum, on the shores of Galilee. The village of Nain was only five miles from Nazareth. In those days, they did not have a closed casket.

35

The dead person was wrapped in a linen sheet and laid on a sort of wickerwork stretcher.

If the family was poor, there would be at least two flute players and one hired mourner. If the family was more well-to-do, there would be many flute players and hired mourners. This widow was apparently loved by the people of the town, and almost the whole village was in the procession.

As they left the village, they met another large procession, the crowd following Jesus. So you see these two companies of people meeting on the narrow pathway, just outside the village of Nain.

One of the first things we notice about how Jesus treats the brokenhearted are His first words to this widow. He said, "Don't weep." What a strange thing for Him to say. People are expected to cry at funerals. Is it wrong to cry at a funeral? No. Jesus Himself cried at the tomb of Lazarus. So what is He saying? He was saying that He felt bad for her. He found His heart touched with her grief. He had compassion on her. "Don't cry." He knew she wouldn't need to cry, for He knew what He was going to do.

Then Jesus did something unusual. He went up and touched the funeral bier. No Jew would have considered such a thing. Those who carried the bier stood still, and the lamentations of the mourners ceased. Can you feel the tension in the air? The company of people gathered about the bier, hoping against hope. One was present who had banished disease and vanquished demons. Was death also subject to His power?

In a clear, authoritative voice, the words are spoken, "Young man, I say unto thee, Arise." Verse 14. That voice pierces the ears of the dead. The young man opens his eyes. Jesus takes him by the hand and lifts him up. His gaze falls upon his mother, and they unite in a long, joyous embrace.

The multitude look on in silence, as if spellbound. Hushed and reverent, they stand for a little time as if in the very presence of God, which indeed they are. Then they begin to glorify God. How would you like to have been there? That was a good funeral!

The second experience is found in the fifth chapter of Mark, and this time a little girl is involved. When a little twelve-year-old girl goes to sleep, somehow that's different than for an older person who has already lived a full three-score years and ten.

Let's begin in Mark 5:22. "Behold, there cometh one of the rulers of the synagogue, Jairus by name; and when he saw him, he fell at his feet, and besought him greatly, saying, My little daughter lieth at the point of death: I pray thee, come and lay thy hands on her, that she may be healed; and she shall live. And Jesus went with him; and much people followed him, and thronged him." Verses 22-24.

As Jesus went with this ruler toward his house, there was an interruption—the woman who touched the hem of His garment was healed and commended for her great faith.

The story continues in verse 35: "While he yet spake, there came from the ruler of the synagogue's house certain which said, Thy daughter is dead: why troublest thou the Master any further?"

Let's not miss the impact of those words. Do you think it's any trouble for Jesus to raise the dead? Do you think it's any problem for the Lifegiver—the One who created us all in the beginning, the One who is keeping our hearts beating right now—do you think it's any trouble for Him to keep going toward the house of Jairus?

But the messenger says, "Don't trouble Him any further."

Just imagine yourself in Jesus' shoes. You have come from the audience chamber of the Most High. You have the assurance from Your Father that He will work through You and that all power in heaven and earth is available to You. You can speak the word, and the little girl will come back to life. Would that be a lot of trouble for you to go and wake her up? No! Instead, it would be a lot of trouble to stay away!

I can remember a funeral for a little grade-school boy. All of his classmates knew he was going to die. The only question was when. One day Hank went to sleep, and we had the funeral there at the church. All of the boys and girls from the school came, and one by one they came down and said Goodbye to Hank.

As I stood there and watched, I remember imagining what it might have been like in the days of Jesus. Oh, how I longed for Him to walk down the aisle, take Hank by the hand, and wake him up.

Jesus could have called attention to Himself. But He was so intent on bringing glory to His Father that He could go into the death chamber, call someone back to life, and then disappear. In fact, He ended up saying, "Don't tell anybody." See verse 43.

If we were able to do something like that, we'd want to make sure it hit the headlines. And that's why we can't do it. Most of us cannot be trusted with the power of God, for it would destroy us.

Well, the messengers said, "Don't trouble the Master any further." And as soon as Jesus heard that, He said to Jairus, "Don't be afraid, only believe." See verse 36. That's how Jesus treated the brokenhearted. He spoke words of comfort and encouragement.

"And he suffered no man to follow him, save Peter, and James, and John the brother of James. And he cometh to the house of the ruler of the synagogue, and seeth the tumult, and them that wept and wailed greatly. And when he was come in, he saith unto them, Why make ye this ado, and weep? the damsel is not dead, but sleepeth." Verses 37-39.

Let's never forget that what we call death, Jesus called sleep.

"And they laughed him to scorn." Verse 40. The flute players and the hired mourners and the neighbors and friends made fun of Jesus. They had seen her lying there on her pallet, silent and still. They said, "Don't try to tell us she's not dead."

"But when he had put them all out, he taketh the father and the mother of the damsel, and them that were with him, and entered in where the damsel was lying. And he took the damsel by the hand, and said unto her, [Little girl], . . . I say unto thee, arise." Verses 40, 41.

Instantly a tremor passes through the unconscious form. The pulses of life beat again. The lips unfold with a smile. The eyes open widely, as if from sleep, and the maiden gazes with wonder on the group beside her.

She arises, and her parents clasp her in their arms and weep for joy. Can you imagine the scene?

The One who treated the brokenhearted like that has promised to come again. He still has the same power over the enemy and over his prison house. He still has the same power to awaken those who sleep and to comfort those who mourn.

The third instance of Jesus' meeting death is found in the story of Mary and Martha and Lazarus recorded in John 11. Jesus loved to visit in the home of these friends of His. Whenever He was in Bethany, He would find some time to spend with them.

But when Lazarus became ill, Jesus was not in town. It was a terrible sickness. The doctor looked serious from the beginning. Things didn't look good. So Mary and Martha sent a messenger off to find Jesus. It was a big project, but they found Him. And when they found Him and told Him about Lazarus's condition, He said, "This sickness is not unto death." Verse 4.

The messenger returned to Bethany and said, "We've got good news. Jesus says that Lazarus's sickness is not unto death." And the sisters rushed into the room of Lazarus and said, "Lazarus, you don't need to worry. We got word from Jesus. You're not going to die."

"Really?"

"Yes, that's what He told the messenger. You won't die."

"Sure feels like it!"

And he continued to hope, but he continued to get worse. Finally he went into a coma—and then he died. It must have been hard for Mary and Martha to accept. What a test of their faith in Jesus!

Back where Jesus was, He said to His disciples, "We're going to go back now, because Lazarus is asleep." See verse 11.

And they said, "Asleep?"

"Yes, he's asleep."

Now the disciples were worried because they had already heard that the people near Jerusalem were out for Jesus' life. There was a plot on His life, and they figured that if they went back with Him, they would be involved in the same plot. Afraid for their own skins, they said, "Let's not go back there. If Lazarus is asleep, after he's been so sick, that's good. Let him sleep.

He needs the sleep. Let's stay here." See verses 8-12.

Jesus said, "I am going back, and I am going to wake him out of sleep."

"Oh no, don't do that!"

And at that point, Jesus finally, reluctantly said what we usually say. Don't miss it, please. Jesus didn't like the word *death*. He didn't call it death. Jesus said, finally, "Our friend Lazarus is dead." But He preferred to call it sleep, and I like that word better too. Because when you sleep, it's not all bad. When you sleep, there is the waking-up time. See verse 14.

When you see a loved one who believes in Jesus but who doesn't have much longer to live, you can join Jesus in saying, "This sickness is not unto death." For the believer, death is a small matter. The time of mourning can be changed to a time of rejoicing when the loved one has fallen asleep in Jesus. We do not sorrow as those who have no hope, for we know that the one who is asleep in Jesus is soon to be awakened.

As we look beyond today, the times of mourning lose their sting. We look forward to the time when Jesus comes to awake those who sleep. Here in the middle of the story of Lazarus we find the famous verse, "I am the resurrection, and the life: he that believeth in me, though he were dead, yet shall he live: And whosoever liveth and believeth in me shall never die. Believest thou this?" Verses 25, 26.

Could I ask the same question today? Jesus said, Whoever liveth and believeth in me shall never die. Do you believe that? Those who do believe it can have good funerals, even though they might weep. For we often weep when we say Goodbye, even when friends leave for a long journey. It's all right to weep. But we don't weep like those who have no hope. See 1 Thessalonians 4:13.

Well, Jesus went out to the cemetery with Mary and Martha, and the crowd followed them. He walked up to the door of the rock-hewn tomb, and He said, "Remove the stone. Roll away the stone."

Even Martha drew back and said, "No, you're going too far."

Jesus had said that Lazarus was sleeping. But by the time the stone was removed, he had been asleep for four days. Nobody could argue this time about whether or not he was really dead.

But they rolled away the stone and watched breathlessly while Jesus prayed a simple prayer. And then Jesus commanded, "Lazarus, come forth!" Verse 43.

Some have said that if He hadn't singled out Lazarus, the entire cemetery would have come alive! Maybe that's true. But Lazarus came forth and was restored to his family and friends. What a story!

We can rejoice today for the good news that what we call death is only sleep—and that Christ still has the power to awaken us from sleep and to give life everlasting. We can rejoice that He still has power over death and the grave. While He comforts us in our times of mourning, He invites us to look forward to the day when He comes again and death is swallowed up in victory.

How Jesus Treated Known Sinners

When I was a little boy, I sat me down to cry,
Because my little brother had the biggest piece of pie.

My father used to quote that verse to my brother and me. At times we needed to hear it!

One year some nice church members gave my brother and me each a bag of Christmas candy, the hard candy that stays in your mouth for hours. My folks were immediately concerned. They didn't want us to ruin our teeth or our stomachs. So they made a rule. Only one piece of candy at a time—and that at mealtimes. No candy between meals.

Well, that was too much for a little guy. So I got into my bag of candy between meals. My father heard about it and promptly destroyed my bag of candy. And at that point I became so concerned about my brother's health that I dumped his bag of candy down the toilet!

Why do we do this kind of thing? Why do we try so hard to keep ahead of each other, whether in the extreme manifestation of war, or in the more innocent parlor games? What makes football—and other sports—such a national pastime? Why do we rally so completely around the question of who's going to win, who's going to be on top, who's going to be first?

It all started with sin, did it not? It all started when Lucifer decided he wanted to be the greatest. It seems to be ingrained in our very natures. Even the disciples of Jesus were guilty again and again of this tendency to want to be the greatest.

Looking into their experience, we are given a beautiful example of how Jesus treated known sinners.

Is it possible for saints to sin? How does Jesus treat saints who sin? Is it possible to sin and to know you are sinning and keep on doing what you're doing wrong, and still be a Christian? I would suggest that this is a very practical question. And it's a question that has an answer so exciting I can hardly wait to present it! But let's try to build our case, as we notice from Scripture how Jesus treated these kinds of people.

"He came to Capernaum: and being in the house he asked them, What was it that ye disputed among yourselves by the way? But they held their peace: for by the way they had disputed among themselves, who should be the greatest." Mark 9:33, 34.

The time had come that Jesus had set His face toward Jerusalem. The disciples were certain the time had come for Him to set up His kingdom—His earthly kingdom. And they had unfinished business they needed to take care of. Their unfinished business was to decide who was going to be president of the class, who was going to be prime minister, who was going to be greatest in the kingdom.

The disciples continued their discussion along the road to Jerusalem, taking care of their unfinished business. But they knew what they were doing was wrong, because they lagged behind Jesus. In fact, by the time Jesus reached the city limits of Capernaum, His disciples were so far behind that He couldn't even hear what they were saying.

It's almost funny. These disciples had been with Jesus for three years. They had repeatedly declared their faith in Him, that He was the Son of God. Yet here you see them trying to speak softly enough that *God* can't hear them!

This teaches us something very interesting about sinning. It's hard to sin in the presence of Jesus. Have you discovered that yet? Even the weakest people find it difficult to sin in the presence of someone they love and respect. And somehow we have to feel that we're away from God, away from Jesus, in order to continue sinning.

But the disciples arrive at Capernaum, and they go with

Jesus to the house where they will be staying. When Jesus found a quiet moment, He asked, "What were you talking about, back there on the road?"

The disciples began to kick their feet in the dust. They began to fidget. And they didn't answer. The Bible says, "They held their peace." It was a good time to hold their peace! When my parents asked me what happened to my brother's bag of Christmas candy, I held my peace!

But Jesus continued to press His point, and at long last one of the disciples said, "Well, uh, ahem—we were wondering who is going to be the greatest in the kingdom."

Now Jesus' life was a life of humility. He had emptied Himself and made Himself of no reputation, according to Philippians 2. He who had received the homage and worship of all the heavenly hosts had come to be born in a stable. He who had been rich had become poor, that we through His poverty might become rich. Again and again He had tried to get the point through to the disciples that real greatness is based upon humility. And they hadn't gotten the message.

At this point, it seems Jesus might have said, "Get out of My sight, you miserable twelve. Give Me another twelve to start over with."

But instead, He sat down with them and said, "If any man desire to be first, the same shall be last of all, and servant of all. And he took a child, and set him in the midst of them: and when he had taken him in his arms, he said unto them, Whosoever shall receive one of such children in my name, receiveth me: and whosoever shall receive me, receiveth not me, but him that sent me." Mark 9:35-37. Jesus was always using little children to show what the kingdom of heaven is really like.

Jesus was kind to His disciples. He didn't condemn them. He continued patiently trying to teach them the lessons they needed so much to learn. Above all, He continued to walk with them, to fellowship with them. He continued to work with them, to travel with them, to trust them with His work and His mission.

From this Scripture lesson we see that the disciples were guilty of sin. What sin? The sin of pride. Oh, we say, everybody has a bit of pride. That's what our world is based on. That's what makes a game of Monopoly fun! And sanctification is the work of a lifetime. Perhaps before we die we'll get on top of that little problem.

But if you study it, you discover that pride is one of the worst sins in God's eyes. Pride is one of the most offensive to God because it is so contrary to His very nature. And pride was the sin that began this whole mess in the first place.

So the sin of which the disciples were guilty was not only sin, it was a bad sin. And they knew it was wrong, and they knew what they were doing, but they kept right on doing it. They continued doing it the whole time they walked with Jesus. In fact, they were still at it the night of the Last Supper in the upper room just before the crucifixion. That qualifies in my definition as known sin, continuing sin, habitual sin, cherished sin, persistent sin.

This Scripture teaches us how Jesus treats sinning sinners—who know they are sinning and yet keep right on sinning.

Someone has said that the problem with these disciples is that they were unconverted. But they had been sent out to cast out devils and cleanse lepers and raise the dead. Do unconverted people do that?

These were the ones to whom Jesus said—when they came back from their mission with the seventy—"Rejoice, because your names are written in heaven." See Luke 10:20. But John 3:3 says you can't even see the kingdom of heaven unless you are born again. So I cannot accept the premise that these disciples were unconverted. What then?

How does Jesus treat disciples who are guilty of known sinning? He made His classic statement in Matthew 12:31: "All manner of sin . . . shall be forgiven unto men." Is that good news? And if all manner of sin shall be forgiven, then this would have to include known sin, persistent sin, habitual sin. It would include forgiveness of the worst sins, such as pride, as well as other sins, such as murder and adultery and you name it.

Jesus offered forgiveness for all sin, and He continued to walk with the disciples as they learned what He was trying to teach them.

It might be easy to conclude that perhaps sinning is not so bad, after all. Maybe sinning is no big deal. Maybe obedience and overcoming are not necessary or even possible. But we need to remember what Jesus said to Mary when she was dragged to Him. He said, "I don't condemn you." That's good news.

But He didn't stop there. What else did He say? He said, "Go and sin no more." That is equally good news.

God loves sinners, it is true. But He hates sin. He has provided power to overcome sin. He has provided power to obey—power to be victorious. And He has also provided forgiveness for weak, immature, growing Christians—and He continues to walk with them.

Power is available to go and sin no more. But it is the acceptance and love of Jesus, the continuing relationship with Him, that brings us this power to go and sin no more. That's why it is an absolute necessity for any sinning sinner to be able to count on the accepting presence of Jesus as he is still learning how to experience the power that is available.

The only person who grows out of his mistakes is the one who knows he's loved and accepted even while he's making them. Does this lead to license? No! It is this very relationship with Jesus that leads to victory.

On the basis of this Bible story, we can conclude that it is possible to have a relationship with God going on and to have a known sin going on in your life at the same time. The disciples had a relationship with God going on and a known sin going on at the same time—true or false?

But even though it is possible to have a relationship with God and a known sin going on at the same time, sooner or later one of the two is going to go.

Judas was the smart one. He understood this principle. He decided he didn't want his sin to go, so he deliberately scrapped his relationship with Jesus in favor of the sin.

Now we have come to the real issue in cherished sin, presumptuous sin, known sin. Judas understood what to do to overcome sin, and he deliberately chose not to do it. And when someone scraps a relationship with Jesus in favor of continuing in sin, he is on exceedingly dangerous ground. Perhaps you have met people who didn't want to get too religious, because they were afraid their life-style would change. Such was the case with Judas.

But the rest of the disciples wanted to stay with Jesus regardless. John, for example. He was the disciple who was always there. Nothing could take him from the side of Jesus. Yet it still took him three years to learn how to accept the victory Jesus had to offer. And in spite of his problems, which were fully as bad as those of Judas, he continued to walk with Jesus.

Years go by. John is the last one left—the last of the disciples. All the rest have died a martyr's death. Perhaps friends come to visit him there in Rome. They hear him say things like, "Beloved, let us love one another: for love is of God." 1 John 4:7.

And they say, "John, you've changed."

John looks at them and asks, "Who, me?"

Because the people who do change are the last ones to know it—the last ones to advertise it. But the grace of God had been doing its work in John. John had been known as one of the "sons of thunder," but now he says, "Beloved, now are we the sons of God, and it doth not yet appear what we shall be: but we know that, when he shall appear, we shall be like him; for we shall see him as he is." 1 John 3:2.

Please, my friend, may I remind you that if you continue to know Jesus as your personal Friend day by day—by prayer and by study of His Word—if nothing takes you from His side, you will join John the beloved in experiencing a transformation of character. Whatever sin you struggle with, it will fade away.

Sometimes we get impatient and try to put timetables on our growth. We'd better not. That's God's department. That's the Holy Spirit's work. The principle of Christian growth is first the blade, then the ear, then the full corn in the ear. It takes time to grow fruit.

But love has its own built-in safeguard against license. The more we love, the further we go from wanting to play cheap and loose with God's grace. And while we grow, while we learn with the disciples to love and trust Him fully, how thankful we can be for the message of how Jesus treated known sinners.

How Jesus Treated the Demon-Possessed

The choir had just finished singing the morning's anthem. With a soft rustle of robes, the singers returned to their places in the choir loft and sat down. A slight stir ran through the congregation as people shifted in their seats, seeking the most comfortable position to sit out the sermon.

The church was crowded that morning, and suppressed excitement was in the air, for the morning speaker had a reputation for being controversial. He wasn't often invited to express His views publicly, and rumor had it that one such service had actually ended in a near riot. The platform elder was understandably a bit nervous as he glanced toward the guest speaker and nodded slightly to indicate that the time had come for Him to begin.

The speaker had scarcely reached the podium and opened His mouth to speak, when the doors to the rear of the sanctuary crashed open. Shrieking and staggering up the center aisle, a demoniac hurled himself into the presence of Jesus. You can read about it in Luke 4:33-36. "In the synagogue there was a man, which had a spirit of an unclean devil, and cried out with a loud voice."

The description is a bit humorous—"an *unclean* devil"! After all, how many *clean* devils are there? But at least we can assume that as devils go, this particular devil was apparently a bad one.

The demoniac "cried out with a loud voice, saying, Let us alone; what have we to do with thee, thou Jesus of Nazareth?

48

art thou come to destroy us? I know thee who thou art; the Holy One of God."

Notice the pronouns—they are very interesting. "Let *us* alone." "What have *we* to do with thee?" "Art thou come to destroy *us?*" Evidently the demon began by speaking both for himself and for the man that he possessed. But then he ended with, "*I* know thee." Perhaps the man did not realize in whose presence he had been so violently placed. But the demon certainly recognized who he was confronting.

This must have been a rather nervy demon. Perhaps he felt especially adventurous that day when he decided to interrupt the church service where Jesus—the One who had created him—was holding forth. But nervy or not, he also must not have been particularly smart. He should have known better, because he ended up in defeat—as the demons always do in the presence of Jesus. For "Jesus rebuked him, saying, Hold thy peace, and come out of him. And when the devil had thrown him in the midst, he came out of him, and hurt him not. And they were all amazed, and spake among themselves, saying, What a word is this! for with authority and power he commandeth the unclean spirits, and they come out."

In the Bible there are seven recorded instances of Jesus' confrontations with the demons. Before we go on to consider the second occasion, please notice three things:

1. Jesus' contact and conversation with the demon was brief.
2. The demon was forced to leave his victim immediately.
3. At least in this particular case, no intercessor was present.

No one was involved in bringing the afflicted man to Jesus or in seeking Jesus' help in his behalf. He came alone. In fact, he wasn't even capable of asking help for himself, for when he tried to speak, the demon spoke through him. Yet Jesus was still able to deliver and save him.

The second case history, Matthew 9:32-34, is very short. "As they went out, behold, they brought to him a dumb man possessed with a devil. And when the devil was cast out, the dumb spake: and the multitudes marvelled, saying, It was never so seen in Israel."

In this case there was intercession, for it says, "*They* brought to him a dumb man possessed with a devil." Once again, however, the encounter was brief. And the evidence is that the demons were forced to leave immediately at Jesus' word. The people who brought this man to Jesus couldn't do anything to help him. But they knew enough to bring him to Jesus, and that's the right thing to do, don't you think? Anyone today who knows someone who is tormented or oppressed or in trouble could follow the example of these people in bringing that one to Jesus. He is the only One who has the power to bring healing and restoration.

Case history number three is found in Matthew 12. "Then was brought unto him one possessed with a devil, blind, and dumb: and he healed him, insomuch that the blind and dumb both spake and saw." Verse 22.

The record continues with a dialogue between Jesus and the Pharisees. But Jesus' actual encounter with the demons again was brief and again ended in their total defeat. The religious leaders accused Jesus of casting out devils by the power of the devil. In return, Jesus gave them some hard-to-answer arguments and told a parable about an empty house—swept and garnished—where many demons returned to take the place of one. We'll come back to this, but for now let's continue to the fourth case history.

This is one of the best-known encounters—the demoniacs who were set free and the demons who drove the pigs over the cliff into the sea. It is recorded in Matthew 8 and Luke 8. In this instance, Jesus engaged in a brief dialogue with the demons. According to Luke 8, He asked, "What is your name?"

And they replied, "Our name is Legion." See verse 30.

In the days of Christ, the Roman army was divided into legions. Each legion was composed of from three to five thousand men. Apparently the devil had enough spare demons that he could waste three to five thousand of them on one or two men!

A popular approach to the subject of exorcism says that you have to talk to each individual demon and weasel them out one by one. If Jesus had used that method in this experience, He would probably still be there!

So although there is Bible evidence for multiple possession, there is no evidence that each demon must be dealt with individually. When Jesus gave the command, they *all* left. A package deal, if you please. The devils went into the swine, the swine ran into the sea, and the people came out and pleaded for Jesus to leave their country before they lost any more of their resources.

In this case, there was no intercessor. Once again the demons exhibited a lack of judgment, or perhaps a lack of self-control, by coming into the presence of Jesus voluntarily. But they were perceptive enough to say, as recorded in Matthew 8:31, "*If* thou cast us out, suffer us to go away into the herd of swine." They surely must have known what the outcome of the encounter was going to be!

The fifth case history is found in Matthew 15:21-28. This is the story of the Phoenician woman whose faith was so great. She persisted, staying in Jesus' presence for some of the crumbs from the Master's table. Her problem was that her daughter was grievously vexed with a devil. At the conclusion of the conversation, Jesus said, "O woman, great is thy faith: be it unto thee even as thou wilt." Matthew concludes his account of this miracle by saying, "And her daughter was made whole from that very hour."

There was an intercessor in this account, but the daughter who was possessed wasn't even present. She received deliverance in absentia, we might say. But even though she was not in His immediate presence, she was delivered immediately at His word.

Case history number six is found in Mark 9:14-29. It's a long one. Jesus has come down from the mount of transfiguration. He had taken three of His disciples on a special trip. The other nine were jealous and had been bickering among themselves about who was going to be the greatest. In that state, they tried to take on the demons, but instead, the demons took them. Although Jesus never lost a case, His disciples did.

When Jesus arrived on the scene, the boy's father explained

the situation to Him, and said, "*If* you can do anything—"

Jesus replied, "All things are possible to him that believes."

Then the man answered, "I believe, but evidently I don't believe enough. Please help me with my unbelief."

Jesus raised up the boy, and there was a great deliverance that day.

After the crowds had melted away, the disciples asked Jesus why they hadn't been able to cast out the demons themselves. And Jesus said, "This kind doesn't come out except by prayer and fasting."

But Jesus, who cast the demon out, hadn't been fasting, so far as we know. It's easy to take a literal interpretation of this and think that God is somehow impressed if we deprive ourselves of food. But this doesn't line up with what Jesus said about God's being *willing* to give good gifts to His children. God's gifts are not earned—they are given freely. So what did Jesus mean?

Jesus was speaking of the continuing relationship with His Father. He didn't try to rein Himself up to some kind of spiritual high just for this occasion. Rather, He spent time every day in communion and fellowship with His Father. This was more important to Him than eating. It was through this relationship that He was kept under His Father's control and was ready at a moment's notice for whatever devices of the devil He might be called upon to face.

On the other hand, His disciples had not spent the night, or the early morning, in fellowship with Heaven as He had. They had fallen asleep while arguing and scrapping among themselves about who was to be the greatest. By their own choice they had separated themselves from the power of heaven and were thus left to meet the enemy in their own feeble strength.

If at any time we try to grapple with the powers of darkness on our own, we will surely be overcome. Unless we have the power of Jesus, it is sheer folly even to attempt a confrontation with the devil. He is stronger than we are, and he will come out on top every time. Only the power of Jesus is strong enough to overcome the enemy, and this power is available to each of us through a daily relationship with Him.

Not only are we incapable of dealing with devil possession in its most extreme form, but we are also incapable of dealing with the devil's temptations and tricks in our own lives. We cannot overcome sin in our own strength, but only through the strength of heaven, as we come to Jesus and allow Him to fight for us.

Finally, case history number seven—found in Mark 16:9. Here we don't have a story, as in the other instances. We have only a reference to something that has already happened.

"When Jesus was risen early the first day of the week, he appeared first to Mary Magdalene, out of whom he had cast seven devils."

We could probably speculate on this, as to whether Jesus cast out seven devils all at once, or cast devils out of Mary seven different times. I'm choosing the latter possibility, because of the parable Jesus told in Matthew 12. Let's go back there, to verses 43-45.

"When the unclean spirit is gone out of a man, he walketh through dry places, seeking rest, and findeth none. Then he saith, I will return into my house from whence I came out; and when he is come, he findeth it empty, swept, and garnished. Then goeth he, and taketh with himself seven other spirits more wicked than himself, and they enter in and dwell there: and the last state of that man is worse than the first. Even so shall it be also unto this wicked generation."

What is Jesus saying? That there's something more important than getting the devil cast out of you. It is also necessary to keep him out. Isn't that true? And Mary had to learn that— evidently the hard way.

A person may know a mighty deliverance from sin—even from devil possession—but unless he knows a vital connection with God and a continuing fellowship with Him day by day, through Bible study and prayer, it's not going to be enough.

Sin is never stamped out by us. It is crowded out when Jesus comes in.

We can draw several conclusions from the study of these case histories. First, when Jesus cast out the devils, He cast them out immediately. Second, He cast all the demons out at once, not one at a time. Third, sometimes there was an intercessor, sometimes not. Evidently it is not essential to have an intercessor. And fourth, casting out devils is no big deal!

In Luke 10, when the seventy returned and said, "Lord, even the devils are subject unto us through thy name," Jesus said, essentially, "*So?* Satan was cast out of heaven a long time ago. He is a defeated foe." See verses 17-20.

How Jesus treated the demon-possessed is good news. It was good news in Palestine; it is good news today. Jesus never lost a case. The devils screamed for mercy in His presence. Therefore, they are nothing to be afraid of, for the mighty name of Jesus is still the greatest power on earth. Through His power, we may be delivered from the power of the enemy.

How Jesus Treated the Poor

A friend of mine and his son were driving along the hot highway in California several years ago, and they passed an ice-cream stand. My friend decided his little ten-year-old boy could use an ice-cream cone. So he stopped the car, gave his boy a dime, and told him to run over and get an ice-cream cone.

In a moment, the boy came back from the ice-cream stand near tears. He still had the dime, and he told his father the man wouldn't sell him an ice-cream cone. So the father got out of the car, went over to the man, and asked, "What's the matter here? Why won't you sell my boy an ice-cream cone?"

The owner of the ice-cream stand said, "We don't sell nine-cent ice-cream cones. Your boy wanted a nine-cent ice-cream cone."

Then it dawned on my pastor friend that his ten-year-old boy had already dedicated his tithe from the dime to the Lord, between the car and the ice-cream stand. So he relaxed, explained to the proprietor of the place what had happened, and apologized for the misunderstanding.

The man said, "Is that what you do with the penny from your dime? You give it to the Lord? Well," he said, "I'll tell you what you do, son. You give *all* of your dime to the Lord, and I'll give you an ice-cream cone." And he put on one scoop, two scoops, three scoops—until the ice cream was running down—and handed it to the boy. Once again the promise was fulfilled that God would open the windows of heaven and pour out a blessing. God delights to honor those who honor Him.

In Mark 12 is a story about how Jesus treated the poor—those who had very little but chose to put God first in their giving. The story begins in verse 41: "Jesus sat over against the treasury, and beheld how the people cast money into the treasury."

You may recall that in the days of Christ, apparently the customary way of receiving offerings was to place a container out in the foyer. And as the people left the church, they put in their offerings. I personally wish we could revive that method for taking the offering! But, nonetheless, that was the method in the days of Jesus.

Jesus was able to be there in the foyer and watch. "And many that were rich cast in much. And there came a certain poor widow, and she threw in two mites, which make a farthing." Verses 41, 42.

A mite is worth only a fraction of one of our pennies. Even the penny that my friend's son set aside from his ice-cream-cone dime was worth more than this widow had. But she cast in her offering, and Jesus saw her.

"And he called unto him his disciples, and said unto them, Verily I say unto you, That this poor widow hath cast more in, than all they which have cast into the treasury: for all they did cast in of their abundance; but she of her want did cast in all that she had, even all her living." Verses 43, 44.

This was a poor widow, but I'd like to suggest that this was a *rich* poor widow. The Bible speaks of those who are rich in faith. And if you had to choose between being rich in faith or rich in this world's goods, which would you take? It might be easy to give a quick answer. But which would you really prefer?

This was a rich poor widow, and she got good marks from Jesus Himself—which she must have heard. Apparently Jesus was in such close proximity to her that she was able to hear what went on between Jesus and His disciples.

This encounter took place in the middle of the last week of Jesus' life, just a few days before the crucifixion. It must have brought encouragement to Jesus' heart to see the faith of this woman. And it must have been encouraging to her to hear what Jesus said.

Jesus often gave words of appreciation. From the time He was a child, He was known for speaking words of encouragement and cheer. And this widow must have gone out from the temple with a lighter step, with hope in her heart, with courage for another day, because of her contact with Jesus that day.

Several lessons concerning giving and Bible principles of giving emerge from this story. First of all, our ability to give depends upon three things: the money we have, the possessions we have, and the earning power we have. Sometimes people's money or cash flow gets lost in possessions. In Matthew 19, Jesus told the rich young ruler, "Go sell all that you have, and give." See verse 21. Get rid of some of your investments.

The Bible standard for giving is found in Malachi, where God's method is described. He asks us to give on the percentage plan. Really, that's the only fair way to measure giving. Sometimes we can fool ourselves into thinking we've given a lot, just because we've given more dollars than someone else. But in the story of this widow, we have another principle; God measures our giving, not by the amount of the gift, but by the amount we have left over after we have given. And by His measurement, this woman had given more than all the rest, for she gave all that she had.

Let's take a modern-day illustration. Suppose a college student trying to work his way through school is able to earn $100 extra during the month. According to the Bible principle of tithing, which is 10 percent, he should return to God $10, which really isn't a gift. It's only being honest. It's not being generous. The Bible teaching is that 10 percent of our increase belongs to God anyway.

But if that same student were also to drop a quarter into the offering plate during the month in addition to his tithe, he might not think he had given very much.

Another person, with steady employment and a regular wage, might make $2,000 during the month, pay $200 tithe, and drop $5 into the offering plate. And that person would have given the same amount as the student.

And the person who makes $10,000 in a month, returns $1,000 in tithe, and puts $25 in the offering plate has given the same percent as the student who gave the quarter. That really tells us something about the fairness of God, doesn't it?

It might be possible to misunderstand the lesson of the story of the widow and say, "We should give everything we have to the church."

No, that is not what Jesus is saying—and is not what He expects. It's all right to have something left. Abraham had something left. Abraham was rich. And Abraham got good marks. Others in Scripture had great wealth: Job, David, and Solomon, to name just a few. It is legitimate to have a base from which to make more money, so long as that increase does not eclipse our sense of need and become more important to us than heavenly treasure. David said it well in Psalm 62:10: "If riches increase, set not your heart upon them."

Let's consider another case history—the story of the rich fool. It's found in Luke 12, beginning with verse 16. "He spake a parable unto them, saying, The ground of a certain rich man brought forth plentifully: and he thought within himself, saying, What shall I do, because I have no room where to bestow *my* fruits?" And right there he missed it. Whose fruits were they?

"And he said, This will I do: I will pull down my barns, and build greater; and there will I bestow all my fruits and my goods. And I will say to my soul, Soul, thou hast much goods laid up for many years; take thine ease, eat, drink, and be merry. But God said unto him, Thou fool."

You're a fool, man. You've forgotten who it is that keeps your heart beating. You've forgotten who it is who really owns the fruit and the cattle upon a thousand hills and the gold and silver and all the mines. "This night thy soul shall be required of thee: then whose shall those things be, which thou hast provided? So is he that layeth up treasure for himself, and is not rich toward God." Verses 16-21.

Here you have a contrast with the poor widow. She gave all she had—he kept all he had. What a difference!

It is human nature that the more money you have, the more money you spend. We build bigger barns. Barns? Well, maybe we aren't all into barns. But how easy it is to use our increase for bigger homes, better cars, more expensive vacations—and to forget the needs of the poor, to neglect the Lord's work, to forget who it is who gives the power to get wealth.

Another lesson from how Jesus treated the poor widow is that the poorest, most humble, and unnoticed—by worldly standards—is still of great value in the eyes of Jesus. By the standards and measures of their day, women were second-class citizens. A woman who had lost the companionship of her husband had lost more than just that—she had lost her status in society. And a woman who was a widow and was poor, was among the lowest of all.

The people of Christ's day measured spirituality by wealth and achievements. Even Christ's disciples, when Jesus told them how hard it was for a rich man to enter into the kingdom of heaven, asked, "Who then can be saved?" See Matthew 20:23-25.

It was commonly accepted that the richer you were, the higher you stood in the eyes of heaven and in the eyes of men.

But in this story we see that the ground is level at the foot of the cross. This widow, in her poverty and humility, was able to give more than all the rest, more than all the rich and the honored and the noticed.

This was true not only in the percentage she gave, but also in the results of her gift. Because of the commendation of Jesus on her tiny offering, others have been encouraged to bring the little they have, that otherwise they might have considered too small to be accepted. And while the offerings of the rich Pharisees have long since been forgotten, the two mites of this widow have been the beginning of a stream of little gifts, widening even to this present day.

She gave because she loved, and that's what made the difference. And it is the love of Jesus that makes all of our giving, great or small, of value in the eyes of heaven.

Our giving is to be a response to, and a reflection of, the gift of Jesus. "For ye know the grace of our Lord Jesus Christ, that, though he was rich, yet for your sakes he became poor, that ye through his poverty might be rich." 2 Corinthians 8:9.

How thankful we can be for the riches that are ours in Christ Jesus. And how thankful we can be for the way He treated the poor widow in giving her eternal riches.

How Jesus Treated Publicans and Tax Collectors

In Luke 19 is found the story of Zacchaeus, who was a wee little man—a wee little man was he. His is an intriguing story. It has all the drama of real life. It has a comical side. And it has a deeply spiritual invitation to a true seeker after God.

"Jesus entered and passed through Jericho. And, behold, there was a man named Zacchaeus, which was the chief among the publicans, and he was rich. And he sought to see Jesus who he was; and could not for the press, because he was little of stature. And he ran before, and climbed up into a sycomore tree to see him: for he was to pass that way. And when Jesus came to the place, he looked up, and saw him, and said unto him, Zacchaeus, make haste, and come down; for to day I must abide at thy house. And he made haste, and came down, and received him joyfully. And when they saw it, they all murmured, saying, That he was gone to be guest with a man that is a sinner. And Zacchaeus stood, and said unto the Lord; Behold, Lord, the half of my goods I give to the poor; and if I have taken any thing from any man by false accusation, I restore him fourfold. And Jesus said unto him, This day is salvation come to this house, forsomuch as he also is a son of Abraham. For the Son of man is come to seek and to save that which was lost." Luke 19:1-10.

Jericho was an interesting city. It has captured the imagination of many boys and girls as the site of the battle of Jericho at the time of Joshua, when the walls came tumbling down. The curse upon Jericho at that time resulted in the old city never being rebuilt. But later another city was built, a modern city, which was the home of Zacchaeus in the days of Jesus.

Jericho was a beautiful city but was known for its publicans and tax collectors. There a Jewish man could turn traitor to his own people, give himself up to the Romans, and thereby make a good living. There a man could become rich, because he was given a portion of his collections. And if his collections were greater, so was his portion. Zacchaeus was not only a publican, he was chief among the publicans. He was the Director of the Internal Revenue Service for the area of Jericho.

But he was little. In spite of his small stature, he had reached the place where he could walk down the city streets of Jericho and cause people to tremble, because of his power and his office and authority. He hardly seemed a likely candidate for the kingdom of heaven, at least by our standards. But he had heard of Jesus. The Holy Spirit had already been working on his heart. And Zacchaeus desperately wanted to see Jesus.

It says he wanted to see who He was—*who* He was. It doesn't say he wanted to see what He did or hear what He said. He wanted to see *who He was*. He wanted to get to the heart of the matter. It's one thing to know something about what Jesus did and what He said. It's another thing to know who He was. The truth of the matter is that much of what Jesus said had been said already in the rabbinical literature. And there were miracles in the days of Elijah and Elisha and the other prophets. Nathanael and Philip, two of Jesus' disciples, had considered Jesus as something more than the son of Joseph from Nazareth. He was the Son of God from heaven. And that made all the difference in the world.

It still does today, doesn't it? Abraham Lincoln did many kind things. We can learn much from the sayings of Confucius or other wise men. Religious leaders of all times have spoken about God. But the thing that gave such force to the words and actions of Jesus was who He was. Zacchaeus, small though he was, seemed to realize this, and he wanted to see for himself who Jesus was.

But he could not see Jesus for the press. This often happened in the days of Christ. In Mark the second chapter we noticed the story of the paralytic who wanted to be healed and to have his sins forgiven. He couldn't get through to Jesus because of the press—because of the crowds. And they finally had to make a hole in the roof to let him down into the presence of Jesus. In Mark the fifth chapter is the story of the infirm woman who wanted only to touch the hem of His garment, but almost missed even that, because of the crowds of people. In Luke the eighth chapter, even Jesus' own mother and brothers were anxious to see Him, but they couldn't get through because of the press.

That can still happen today, can't it? It is possible to be so busy, to be so pressed on every side with the needs of other people, even in doing the work of the Lord, that we forget the Lord of the work. It is possible even in the church that we do not see the Lord because of the press.

And so you see this man Zacchaeus, who ordinarily walked with great dignity down the streets of Jericho, suddenly running with the street urchins for the nearest tree. Obviously, in seeking Jesus he had forgotten himself to a great extent. His need was so great that in seeking for help he lost his usual inhibitions.

This has often happened. I remember hearing about an earthquake in California several years ago. During the middle of the earthquake a man was trying to comfort his hysterical neighbors. He was at the front-yard fence, telling the women and children that they shouldn't scream like that—it was going to be all right.

Then he discovered that all he had on was a pair of shoes. He rushed back to his house and found that the front screen door was still locked from the inside—and there was a hole through the screen where he had come out. He had forgotten all of his inhibitions when life was at stake.

Zacchaeus had one supreme motivation. Jesus was coming to town. He had to see Jesus. He had to see who He was. If there was the slightest chance he could find the solution to the sleepless nights and the guilt and remorse, no way was he going to miss that chance. So he ends up on the limb of a tree overlooking the place where Jesus was about to pass by.

When Jesus stopped underneath the tree, He looked up and

gave Zacchaeus the surprise of his life. Not only did He see him up there in the foliage, but He called him by name. "Zacchaeus, make haste, and come down." Verse 5.

Now this could have been an embarrassing situation. I know a little about it from personal experience. When we were living in Grand Junction, Colorado, several years ago, a rodeo came to town. Our boy—age ten or twelve at the time— was excited. He wanted to see the rodeo.

In Grand Junction, Colorado, the rodeo is sort of like a downtown bake sale—you know, the biggest small-town happening of the year. Everybody was going to the rodeo, including many of my church members. However, I wasn't sure that all of my church members would want their pastor to go. But my boy wanted to go to the rodeo. So finally we decided to go to the rodeo grounds together and climb one of the trees next to the fence and watch from there.

I didn't expect to see other church members there in the trees! But to my surprise, no sooner were we settled where we could get a view of the rodeo, when some juniors in the next tree recognized us and said, "Why, *Pastor Venden*—!"

I had lost my inhibitions in my concern for my boy and his desire to see the rodeo. But suddenly I got my inhibitions back again and found it very embarrassing.

Zacchaeus was so intent on seeing Jesus and who He was that apparently he didn't even find it embarrassing to be discovered up there with the street urchins. In spite of the crowd looking on, the Bible says he responded joyfully and made haste and came down. The one big opportunity of his life had come.

He made haste and came down. Isaiah said it in Isaiah 57:15: I dwell with the one "that is of a contrite and humble spirit." Jesus said it: "Blessed are the poor in spirit: for their's is the kingdom of heaven." Matthew 5:3.

Zacchaeus was up a tree for more than one reason. He was there not only physically, but spiritually. And Jesus invited him to come down to bow low at the foot of the cross, acknowledging his great need.

Zacchaeus came down. He didn't belong up in the tree. Someone else belonged on the tree, and He was nailed to the tree not long after.

Zacchaeus received Jesus joyfully. And when that happened, the crowd began to murmur and complain. They said that Jesus had gone to be a guest with a man who was a sinner. Why did He have to choose this wretch to have lunch with? Weren't there respectable and influential people in the city of Jericho to whose homes Jesus could have gone?

The crowds complained about the same thing another time, when they said, "This man receiveth sinners, and eateth with them." Luke 15:2. But that's good news. That's the gospel in one sentence. If not for the fact that Jesus receives sinners and eats with them, there would be no hope for you or me today. Aren't you glad that He is willing to be the guest of people who are sinners?

Right here comes a strange departure in the story—one that has often bothered some of us. Zacchaeus evidently began beating his own moral drums. He "stood, and said unto the Lord; Behold, Lord, the half of my goods I give to the poor; and if I have taken any thing from any man by false accusation, I restore him fourfold." Luke 19:8. What was he doing? Well, some might say he was trying to earn his salvation. But notice Jesus' reply. Jesus said, "This day is salvation come to this house." Verse 9.

Zacchaeus didn't have to wait until he had covered his tracks and given 50 percent, and restored 400 percent. No, salvation wasn't in that. Salvation came on the day when he received Jesus into his house and into his heart. It is when Christ is received as a personal Saviour that salvation comes to the soul.

And the desire on the part of Zacchaeus to restore and to give to those in need was an indication that he had already accepted this salvation—it was not a step in earning salvation. Is there a difference? It was the result of salvation, not the cause. That day—the day Zacchaeus accepted Jesus—salvation came to his house.

But what about the next day? There is another key phrase in this story. Jesus said, "Today I must abide at your house." See verse 5. Once you have accepted salvation, once you come down from your high perch, once you've let Jesus be the One to be lifted up, you must still hear anew every day those familiar words. Make haste today—make haste tomorrow—make haste every day to come down and to let Jesus abide at your house.

It is not enough to accept Him once only, no matter how great your need. Jesus wants to abide with us—to stay with us. In Revelation 3:20 He says, "Behold, I stand at the door, and knock: if any man hear my voice, and open the door, I will come in to him, and will sup with him, and he with me." Jesus is still saying, Today I want to abide at *your* house, in *your* heart, in *your* life.

How Jesus Treated Outsiders

A Jewish doctor in Los Angeles was on the staff of a hospital owned by a Protestant denomination. One time he told of his experiences in being an outsider and becoming an insider. He said he was about ready to graduate from his specialty in medicine, and one part of the final examination was to go into the room of a patient he had never seen before and come out within minutes with a diagnosis. The patients had been well coached not to disclose their illness.

So this Jewish doctor went into the room assigned to him, and here was a woman in the bed. He thought he might as well shoot for the moon to begin with, so he said, "What do you have?"

She said, "You're the doctor—you find out."

So he began his examination. After a few moments he asked her to turn over, and she turned about an inch.

He said, "I beg your pardon, I'd like to have you turn over." And she turned another inch.

At that point he broke into some select Yiddish words, not realizing that his patient was also Jewish. She looked up at him and asked, "Are you Jewish?"

He said, "Yes."

She said, "I've got diabetes!"

And he said he had never felt so "in" in his life!

Whether you're talking about medical practice or about the church or about the world at large, it's possible to be an insider—or an outsider. In fact, if we were to exercise our minds just a bit, we would probably see that it is possible to be an insider, even though you're on the outside; or to be an outsider when you're on the inside!

With that in mind, it is intriguing to notice how Jesus treated the "outsiders" in His day, to discover who the "insiders" really are.

"A certain centurion's servant, who was dear unto him, was sick, and ready to die. And when he heard of Jesus, he sent unto him the elders of the Jews, beseeching him that he would come and heal his servant. And when they came to Jesus, they besought him instantly, saying, That he was worthy for whom he should do this: for he loveth our nation, and he hath built us a synagogue.

"Then Jesus went with them. And when he was now not far from the house, the centurion sent friends to him, saying unto him, Lord, trouble not thyself: for I am not worthy that thou shouldest enter under my roof: Wherefore neither thought I myself worthy to come unto thee: but say in a word, and my servant shall be healed. For I also am a man set under authority, having under me soldiers, and I say unto one, Go, and he goeth; and to another, Come, and he cometh; and to my servant, Do this, and he doeth it." (Notice this centurion had also said to the Jewish rulers, Go, and they had gone!)

"When Jesus heard these things, he marvelled at him, and turned him about, and said unto the people that followed him, I say unto you, I have not found so great faith, no, not in Israel. And they that were sent, returning to the house, found the servant whole that had been sick." Luke 7:2-10.

Jesus marveled at the centurion's faith. The gospels mention two specific times when Jesus marveled—or wondered—and for opposite reasons. Here, He marveled at the faith of an outsider. In the other case, He marveled at the lack of faith of the insiders—the religious people of His day.

I suppose you have heard of the seven wonders of the world. The last time I checked there were about 280 of them! But let's consider seven wonders from this story—seven things we might wonder or marvel at, as we consider this experience.

The first concerns the centurion who sent word to Jesus

about his servant who was ill. Isn't it a wonder that a Gentile—considered a dog by the religious people of that day—would even have the courage to do what he did? Gentiles were outsiders. They were not even considered as worthy of God's notice, blessing, or salvation. So he must have possessed a truly marvelous degree of faith even to try breaking through the Jewish system.

Not only was he a Gentile; he was a Roman. The Romans in the days of Christ were the kind of people who would stop you on the street if it were cold and insist you give them your coat. If a Roman had a heavy load to carry, he would force some Jew to carry it for him. Roman soldiers were not known for their kindness, courtesy, or virtues. And not only was this man a Roman soldier, he was a centurion, in charge of a hundred men in the Roman army. What an unlikely candidate for one of great faith.

The second thing we could wonder about in this story is the fact that this centurion was a Christian. Evidently his faith came from a personal experience with God, and he knew something about God, even before he met Jesus. In fact, he knew enough about God that he recognized Jesus as God. Even the Jewish people of that day didn't do that. They were so busy being good, externally, that they didn't have any time to realize who this Galilean was. But the centurion knew.

He said, "I have authority." And he went on to describe the limits of the authority he had. But he saw himself as only a reflection in the presence of the One who had all power in heaven and on earth. He recognized in Jesus the One who had authority; his faith accepted Jesus as One sent from God. He apparently had no question about it, and all the religious people of his day could have joined him, if they had so chosen.

The third thing I'd like to invite you to marvel at, concerning this centurion, is that he asked for no sign. People in those days were always asking for signs. "Show us a sign, and then we will believe." Jesus told them one time, "You wouldn't believe even if one were to rise from the dead."

Later He proved His point by raising Lazarus from the dead, and not only did they not believe, they plotted to kill both Jesus and Lazarus—the one He had raised from the dead. The sign made no difference.

To the Jewish nobleman who came to Jesus, He said, "Except ye see signs and wonders, ye will not believe." John 4:48. How easy it is to base our trust in God on whether or not we receive the answers we ask for. Jesus saw in the heart of the Jewish nobleman a conditional faith that would not believe unless signs and wonders were produced. But not so with the Roman centurion. He accepted Jesus for who He was, even before the signs and wonders.

A fourth reason why we should wonder at this story is because of the condition of the servant. He was a dying man. The centurion's request was more than asking Jesus to cure a common cold. This man was in deep trouble. He was on his deathbed. Yet the centurion was willing to ask for what looked like the impossible. He believed that the Creator of the universe could speak the word and his servant would be healed.

Are you willing to ask God for something big? Or are you afraid that if you ask for something big it might not happen? Do you have only enough faith to bring to God the small requests? Or do you, with this centurion, bring to God the impossible requests?

A fifth thing we might marvel at is the fact that the centurion's faith went so far as to say to Jesus, Just speak the word. Imagine going to a doctor today in behalf of your loved one's serious health problem. Would you prefer to have him examine your loved one personally, or would you be willing to say, "Just speak the word. Tell us what medicine will cure the problem, and that will be enough."

This man was given a choice of having the Great Physician make a house call or not, and he refused, saying, "That won't be necessary. Just speak the word." That takes a lot of faith, doesn't it?

Right here we can see the spiritual lesson in this story. In looking at physical healing, let's not miss the deeper lesson. We are all aware that not everyone who prays and asks for physical healing is healed of his physical problems today. Even the most godly sometimes suffer and die in this world of sin.

But it is a universal and timeless principle that God is in the business of forgiving sin. And there is no condition, except that we come to Him and ask. In His wisdom, God has a plan which does not include healing everyone of his physical diseases. Otherwise He would have long ago developed a world full of "rice Christians"—people who served Him only for what they could get out of Him. God wants a people who will be faithful unto death, to witness before the universe that they will still love and trust Him no matter what happens.

But when it comes to the forgiveness of sins, He forgives all of our sins, and He does even more. He heals all of our spiritual diseases as well. We go to the Great Physician for more than forgiveness. We go there to get well. And it is His plan that we rise to walk in newness of life. Victory and obedience and overcoming—not merely forgiveness—are available to every one who comes.

It is His will for each of us not only to find forgiveness for our sins when we confess them to Him, but also to be cleansed from all unrighteousness. That is His word, and as we accept His word in faith, we find it fulfilled in the selfsame hour.

A sixth reason to wonder at the centurion is because of his humility. The Jewish leaders who came with his request said to Jesus, He is worthy. He is worthy. If you're looking for someone who is worthy, to whom you want to give your good gifts, we've got one for you. He's built us a synagogue. He deserves an extra blessing for that.

But the centurion sent word, I am *not* worthy. I am not worthy for you to even come under my roof. Speak the word only, and my servant will be healed.

There's a big difference between being worth something and being worthy. We often feel we're not worth anything. That's one of the great problems in the world today. Many people feel worthless. Jesus at the cross proved that we are worth everything. But that doesn't make *us* worthy.

When the centurion said, I am not worthy, he was giving evidence of genuine faith. Genuine faith is trust in another, and when we trust another, we admit that we need another. To admit that we need Jesus day by day is an experience of humility.

But it is only the person who gets low enough at the foot of the cross who can experience the blessings of the cross.

I would like to join the centurion today and say, "Lord, I am not worthy of the least of Your favors, but Jesus left heaven for me." And Jesus proved that we are worth the whole universe, as far as He is concerned.

The seventh reason we might wonder at the centurion today is that, even though he was an outsider—a heathen in the eyes of the Jewish leaders—he had been transformed by God to have a real burden for his servant, for someone else. He said, "Won't you please come and heal him, because he is dear to me." Can you hear an army officer saying that?

Do you have someone who is dear unto you? You can come to Jesus today, and say, "Will You please do something for this person? He's dear unto me—she's dear unto me." That's what makes a real insider—when you have the compassion and spirit of Jesus and are more concerned about others than anything else.

Can you picture in your imagination the conclusion to the story? When Jesus heard about the centurion's servant, He said without hesitation, "I will come and heal him."

Centuries have now gone by, and we're living on the verge of eternity. I can see Jesus today—Jesus who is at the Father's right hand, Jesus who has all power in heaven and in earth. He looks down upon a world in trouble, a world filled with pain and death and tears. And I can hear Him say once again, "I will come. I will come and heal them."

There will come a day very soon now when He will come and heal all of His servants who are dear unto Him. The controversy will be ended. The question of God's love and justice will be forever settled. And Jesus will do what He has wanted to do all along. He will heal all of us—all of us who have accepted His love. God Himself will come to dwell with us and will wipe away all tears. What a beautiful picture. What a beautiful hope. What a beautiful love God has for us.

How Jesus Treated Women

We haven't seen women running jackhammers yet, but women are now truck drivers, gas-station attendants, and police officers. And some people have done a lot of discussing and rethinking concerning the roles of women in the church. If women's rights have merit in other areas, why not have women as pastors and elders?

For those asking these questions, and perhaps for others as well, the subject of how Jesus treated women is very interesting. It should be of interest to at least 50 percent of the readers of this volume—though I'm not just sure which 50 percent!

In recent years, more than one author has described Jesus as a champion of women. Is this true, according to the record of the four Gospels? If He was indeed a champion of women, in what sense was He such, and how did He contend for womanhood?

If we consider the cultural and social aspects of the days of Christ, we will notice that the church leaders—the rabbis—were anything but champions of women's rights. In fact, a prayer that has come out of the rabbinical literature, that may have been used even then, goes something like this:

"Blessed art Thou, O Lord our God, King of the universe, who hast not made me a heathen. Blessed art Thou, O Lord our God, King of the universe, who hast not made me a bondman. Blessed art Thou, O Lord our God, King of the universe, who hast not made me a woman."

The prayer has been changed in recent years—patched up a bit—but those are the kinds of things they said and thought in the days of Christ. Another excerpt from rabbinical literature says, "Happy is he whose children are males, and woe to him whose children are females." Now please—these are not my words! I'm only trying to give a little background from the days of Christ. Certainly it was not the thing in those days to be championing women's rights.

First of all, let's briefly consider the teachings of Jesus. He often referred to women in His stories and parables. We're all familiar with the parable of the woman who put leaven into the loaves of bread—a story explaining the kingdom of heaven. We've heard the parables of the lost sheep, the lost son, and the lost coin—a coin lost by a woman and perhaps part of her dowry. We've heard about the ten bridesmaids in a parable that has significance to the very end of time.

Jesus told a story about a persistent widow, illustrating the importance of persistence in prayer. Jesus spoke of Lot's wife in an illustration, as well as the Queen of Sheba. And we've already noticed in some detail how He commended the widow in the temple who gave her two mites.

In Matthew 21, after the story of the two sons—only one of whom really obeyed his father—Jesus said that even harlots would enter the kingdom of heaven before the religious leaders of His day. In His very first sermon in Nazareth, He made reference to the widow of Zarephath in the days of Elisha. When He talked to His disciples about the second coming, He talked about two women grinding at the mill. Jesus often spoke of women and referred to them in illustrating His teachings.

Now let's consider a few examples of Jesus' actual relationships to women. One writer has analyzed it this way: "In his relationship to women, Jesus' lifestyle was so remarkable that one can only call it astonishing. He treated women as fully human, equal to men in every respect. No word of depreciation about women as such is ever found on His lips. As the Saviour who identified with the oppressed, and the disinherited, He talked to women and about women with complete freedom and candor."

In considering Jesus' relationship to women, let's look first of all at His relationship to His own mother.

When He was twelve years of age, at the time of His first trip to campmeeting at Jerusalem, He was separated from His parents, and they went their way not realizing that He was not with them. When they finally found Him again after searching for three days, they reproved Him. And even at the age of twelve, He said, "Why did you look for Me? Don't you know that I must be about My Father's business?" See Luke 2.

At first glance you might get the idea that He was being a little impudent, maybe. But not so. Because the Gospel record is that He went down with them and was subject to them for the next eighteen years. But the distinct implication here is that Jesus was—perhaps for the first time—realizing a tension and a balance between family loyalty and loyalty to His Father in heaven.

The second reference to Jesus' relationship to His mother appears in the story of the wedding at Cana. They needed more grape juice, as you recall. Jesus' mother came to Him and told Him of their need. And Jesus replied, "Woman, what have you to do with Me?" See John 2.

Many people have thought this was a little rude. But a study of the forms of speech of that day will show that it was not rude. In fact, it could even have been a response of respect. However, there is still the suggestion that while Jesus had respect for His mother, He had to watch carefully the balance between that and the work His Father had sent Him to do.

The third reference is set at Capernaum, where Jesus' mother and brothers tried to see Him but could not get in—the crowds were so great. Instead of interrupting His teaching, He said, "Whoever does the will of God is brother, sister, or mother." Again, He emphasized that God's service cannot take second place—even to the family relationship. And His own mother, blessed among women though she was, could not get into the kingdom of heaven simply because of being His mother. She would need to have her own relationship with God.

The fourth reference to Jesus' relationship with His mother is set at the cross, when He looked down and saw her standing there with John—John, the one who was always there. And He said, "Woman, behold thy son!" and to John, "Behold thy mother!" John 19:26, 27. Thus He showed a tender regard for His mother to the very end.

Now another area of Jesus' relationship with women had to do with the women who were His followers. "It came to pass afterward, that he went throughout every city and village, preaching and shewing the glad tidings of the kingdom of God: and the twelve were with him, and certain women, which had been healed of evil spirits and infirmities, Mary called Magdalene, out of whom went seven devils, and Joanna the wife of Chuza Herod's steward, and Susanna, and many others. [And many others!], which ministered unto him of their substance." Luke 8:1-3.

Jesus' followers consisted of twelve apostles and a band of Galilean women. Why did they follow Him? Did they come by invitation? Jesus told His apostles one time, "You did not choose Me, but I chose you." See John 15:16. It could very well be that Jesus had chosen these women too.

What did they do? They accompanied Him. And you could well speculate on the problem it might have created when they came to a town looking for lodging. They supported Him. There is evidence that some of these women were well-to-do. They accompanied Him to the very end; when the twelve disciples took off on the hundred-yard dash, trying to save their own skins, the women stayed by. And they were the first to receive the message of the resurrection.

Another example of Jesus' relationship to women is His friendship with Mary and Martha. You know the story. It's found in Luke the tenth chapter. There it says that Mary sat at Jesus' feet. What does that mean? In the days of Christ, it was the student who sat at the feet of the teacher. In fact, Martha called Jesus "the Teacher" in John 11, when she gave the word to Mary to come, saying, "The Teacher is here." It was unheard of in the days of Christ for a rabbi to teach a woman. In fact, the rabbis had a saying that it was better to teach a Samaritan than a woman, and you know how they felt about the Samaritans!

But Mary sat at Jesus' feet, and from the lips of her sister Martha came one of the greatest affirmations of Jesus and who

He was. It was at the time when Lazarus had died, and Jesus had just arrived in Bethany. Martha said, "I believe that You are the Christ, the Son of God, He who is coming into the world." See John 11:27. How could you ask for greater faith than that?

Another instance illustrating Jesus' relationship with women occurred when He was anointed. All four of the Gospels record it, and it happened at the feast at Simon's house. What happened there would have been frowned upon by all the Jews of that day—Jesus allowed a woman to touch Him. He allowed a woman *whose hair was let down* to touch Him. (In those days, to let down the hair was something only the women of the streets did.) Not only that, but Jesus said, recording it for all generations, that she had done a beautiful thing.

Then you have Jesus and the Samaritan woman. In the days of Christ, they had a rule which said, "A man shall not be alone with a woman in an inn, not even with his sister or his daughter, on account of what men may think. A man shall not talk with a woman in the street, not even with his own wife, and especially not with another woman, on account of what men may think." Makes you wonder what kind of men they had in those days! But Jesus talked to the woman at the well unashamedly, breaking all Jewish custom.

The experience of Jesus and the adulterous woman who was dragged to Him is also recorded. He stood up for her in the presence of those who were eager to condemn. Why, the experiences of Jesus in relating to women seem to go and on!

What about Jesus' healing of women? He healed Peter's mother-in-law—and on the Sabbath. He broke two rules at the same time, for not only did He heal her on the Sabbath day, but He touched her—He grasped her hand.

Another instance is recorded in Luke 13:10-17—the woman who had been afflicted for eighteen years. Again, she was healed on the Sabbath day, and Jesus laid His hands on her publicly—an absolute no-no among the Jewish people.

Also recorded is the story of the widow's son raised to life at the village of Nain. Jesus interrupted the funeral and brought joy to a troubled heart. When Jairus's daughter was raised,

Jesus again broke all Jewish custom, touching the little girl who was dead and bringing her back to life. On His way to that appointment, a woman in the crowd pressed in to touch the hem of His garment. Jesus stopped and asked, Who touched me? He called this timid woman from her hiding place and affirmed her as a person worthy of healing. He acknowledged her faith and determination. He treated her as a person in her own right.

A last experience of Jesus and His relationship to women happened on the way to Calvary. The women were weeping. They perhaps had not had much contact with Jesus before, but their hearts were touched with His suffering. We ought to have more men like that! Men like Simon from Cyrene, who couldn't keep quiet when he saw a Man suffering under a cross. But the women wept, and Jesus noticed them.

No instance is recorded in the Gospels of a woman ever being hostile to Jesus. Jesus associated freely with, and presented His message to, both men and women. Women were treated as equal in every sense. He chose women as well as men to be His special friends. He graciously accepted their affection and honored it as a beautiful thing. He never hesitated to minister to women. And He demonstrated that it is possible to associate with women on a high, spiritual plane. Thus by His own acceptance of them, He may truly be described as a champion of women.

How Jesus Treated the Hopeless

The city of Jerusalem has been destroyed many times. Many cities and villages of Palestine no longer exist as they did in the time of Christ. Over the years, people have simply built new cities on top of the old ones.

When I toured the Holy Land with some others a few years ago, we went to visit the Pool of Bethesda. It is eighty feet below the surface of the present city, and you can step down the winding stairs to the level of the pool, where it was in the days of Jesus.

When you get down to the five porches, another stair goes down even farther, in the darkness, to the existing waters of the pool. One of our group at that time accidentally disappeared into the pool as he was trying to make his way down the dark staircase. He found that the waters troubled him, instead of the waters being troubled!

But the pool of Bethesda is still there and provides something of a picture of what it was like in the days of Jesus.

The story of the man at the Pool of Bethesda is found in the fifth chapter of John: "After this there was a feast of the Jews; and Jesus went up to Jerusalem. Now there is at Jerusalem by the sheep market a pool, which is called in the Hebrew tongue Bethesda, having five porches. In these lay a great multitude of impotent folk, of blind, halt, withered, waiting for the moving of the water." Then follows a verse not included in your more accurate Bible translations, but here it is in the King James Version: "For an angel went down at a certain season into the pool, and troubled the water: whosoever then first after the troubling of the water stepped in was made whole of whatever disease he had." John 5:1-4.

This was hocus-pocus—the magic of their day. The Lourdes, if you please, where people could go to find health and healing—or at least so they thought.

"And a certain man was there, which had an infirmity thirty and eight years. When Jesus saw him lie, and knew that he had been now a long time in that case, he saith unto him, Wilt thou be made whole? The impotent man answered him, Sir, I have no man, when the water is troubled, to put me into the pool: but while I am coming, another steppeth down before me.

"Jesus saith unto him, Rise, take up thy bed, and walk. And immediately the man was made whole, and took up his bed, and walked: and on the same day was the sabbath." Verses 5-9.

The rest of the chapter deals with the sequel to this story. Jesus was called before the tribunal and arraigned before an earthly court. Jesus, the Lord of the Sabbath, was charged with Sabbath breaking. It might be funny if it weren't so tragic. Jesus—the Creator, the One who made everything, the One who was keeping the hearts beating in the people who were accusing Him. An interesting sight indeed.

On six different occasions Jesus was charged with Sabbath breaking. And as you study these six occasions, you will notice that Jesus always decided in favor of the person, while the religious leaders always decided in favor of the law.

But in Matthew 12:12, Jesus said, "It is lawful to do well on the sabbath days." So Jesus "broke" the Sabbath in order to keep it. And the Jewish leaders, in trying to keep it, ended up breaking it. When Jesus decided in favor of the person, He was really deciding in favor of the law as well. The two are not mutually exclusive. It is lawful to do well on the Sabbath day.

That word *lawful* is very interesting. The text doesn't say, It's nice to do well on the Sabbath day, or It's your privilege to do well. It says it is *lawful* to do well. In other words, that's what the law requires. It's like driving on one of the freeways which has a sign that says, "Minimum speed limit, 40 m.p.h." Not only is it permissible to drive over 40 m.p.h., but you will be breaking the law if you drive slower. To do well on the Sabbath day is what the law requires, and Jesus came to reveal the true purpose of the Sabbath. He apparently cast all caution to the winds, took a giant leap across all tradition and ritual, and showed what true Sabbath keeping was all about.

On this particular Sabbath, Jesus had been wandering through the five porches. The people here were hopeless cases. Their friends or families had brought them here as a last resort. Some had rude shelters erected about the pool; others were brought to the pool on a daily basis. All were waiting for the waters to be troubled so they could try to be first into the pool. The sick and inform and withered and wretched and hopeless were everywhere—waiting.

Jesus walked alone and unnoticed among the suffering ones. It was early in His ministry. Later, the people would crowd Him and follow Him and throng His footsteps. But no crowds followed on this day at the pool, no women pushed through, trying to touch even the hem of His garment.

So Jesus wandered about the five porches looking at the wretched sufferers and longing to heal them. And He wanted to heal them all! If I had been there and recognized Him and known of His power, I would have cried out, "Go ahead, Jesus! Heal them all!"

But He couldn't do it. His mission included many things yet, and if He had healed them all, it would have cut short His work. In fact, by healing just one man, He was to take a giant step toward the cross. That's the reason He didn't heal all the lepers. It would have interfered with His greater mission—the salvation of all mankind.

That's why God didn't bring an end to sin long ago. That's why He can't heal them all today—all the sick and infirm in the hospitals and nursing homes and institutions. God, in His wisdom, has to allow sin to run itself out to its ultimate conclusion so that all will see it for what it really is. And when the end of sin finally does come, no one will have any more stomach for it forever.

But as Jesus wandered about the five porches, longing to heal them all and perhaps looking forward to the day when sin would be forever ended and all *would* be healed, He saw one most wretched case. And His compassion got the better of Him.

Here is a man who has been ill for thirty-eight years. His friends are gone, his family is gone, and his only home is here at the pool. Jesus stops, looks down at him, and asks what would seem to be a foolish question.

"Would you like to be made whole?"

"I beg your pardon? What do you think I'm doing here?"

"Would you like to be made whole?" Evidently He wanted the man to say it.

Well, you know his response. "Yes, that is what I'm after. But there is no one here. I have no man. And I'm not strong enough to get into the pool. Someone else always gets there first. It's hopeless."

Jesus doesn't waste any time. He doesn't mince words. He looks at the man, and with the power that comes from the Life-giver, the Creator, the One who made the universe—the power that caused the dust to jump to attention at creation—He commands, "Rise, take up your bed, and walk."

Now please notice the intriguing sequence here. The record is that (1) immediately the man was made whole, (2) he took up his bed, and (3) he walked.

How easy for us to weave self into the picture. We want just a little credit, just a little glory for ourselves. And we say, God helps those who help themselves. We want God's gifts to be dependent upon our work in some way. Perhaps you have heard people say that the thing which enabled this man to walk was that he set his will and gritted his teeth and determined to do what Jesus said. And as he put forth his effort in that direction, he was made whole and was able to walk. Not so. Jesus healed him on the spot. He was first healed; *then* he got up, picked up his bed, and walked. The walking and the carrying of the bed were results of the healing—not the cause.

And you see this man walking—make that *leaping*—away from the pool. What does the pool represent? The pool represents something we can do to accomplish our own healing. The pool could represent something we try to do to accomplish our salvation or to achieve our victory or our righteousness.

Perhaps a few, whose sickness was in their minds only, were apparently healed because they thought so. But this man was weak. He didn't even have the strength or energy to make it to the pool. He was a hopeless case.

Are you in his shoes? Let's not miss the spiritual lesson from this story. What is your pool today? Have you been trying to earn your way to heaven—trying to be good enough to make it? Is that your pool? You'll never make it on your own.

Have you been trying to obtain the victory over some sin in your life? And have you had no peace? And are you ready to despair? Is that your pool? What about the church members who are trying to do something to cause Christ to come again? Have you ever heard of it? Have you seen the mottos and placards that say, "Let us arise and finish the work"? And then you hear that the world population is growing faster than the gospel is going, and you are ready to give up hope. Is that your pool today?

We have all kinds of pools that we struggle to reach. Perhaps there is someone today who has been trying for thirty-eight years, or even longer, to reach your pool and hasn't made it yet. I have good news for you! "There is a fountain filled with blood, drawn from Immanuel's veins; / And sinners, plunged beneath that flood, lose all their guilty stains." There is a robe for those who are naked, a robe woven without one thread of human devising. It is offered to you today as a gift. It is the robe of Jesus' power in place of your failure.

So would you please join me today on one of these five porches? Jesus is passing by. He bends over you and asks, "Would you like to be made whole?"

Right here, we get into what some people call a subjective gospel. They say, "Don't talk about being made whole. Let's be objective. Let's not look at ourselves."

Can you imagine Jesus bending over this man at the pool and saying, Would you like to be made whole?

And the man says, "Oh, that's too subjective. Just put some righteousness to my account in heaven. That will be enough."

We can be thankful for what Jesus has done at the cross, but we can be equally thankful for what He wants to do in each life today. Charles Spurgeon, the mighty preacher from yesteryear, put it this way: "And now, my dear hearers, I will ask the question of you. Wilt thou be made whole? Do you desire to be saved? Do you know what being saved is? Oh, you say, it is escaping from hell. No, no, no. That is the result of being saved. Being saved is an entirely different thing. Do you want to be saved from the power of sin? Do you desire to be saved from being covetous, worldly-minded, impure, evil tempered, unjust, ungodly, domineering, drunken, or profane? Are you willing to give up the sin that is dearest to you?

"No, says someone, I cannot honestly say I desire all of that. Then you are not the one I am speaking to today.

"But there is one who says, Yes, I long to be rid of sin, root and branch. I desire by God's grace this very day to become a Christian, and to be saved from my sins. Then rise, take up your bed, and walk."

Won't you accept this very best Friend you could ever have, the Lord Jesus Himself, who walks among the five porches? He came not to call the righteous, but sinners to repentance. And He says, "Look unto me, and be ye saved, all the ends of the earth." Isaiah 45:22. He was willing to take the risk for you. His compassion always gets the best of Him. And He offers to you today the spiritual healing you so desire.

How Jesus Treated His Disciples

Have you ever thought of dying for Christ? Would you be willing to? And if you were willing, would you be able to? Surely those who have given their lives for Christ have had to receive help from above.

During the Boxer Rebellion, bandits took a missionary in China to their mountain retreat and tried to force him to give up his faith. He refused. So they cut off all of his fingers and all of his toes. Then they asked, "Now will you give up your faith?"

But he said No. So they cut off his hands at the wrists and his feet at the ankles and shouted at him to renounce his faith in Christ. Still he refused. Finally they cut off his arms and legs, and as he was dying in his own blood, they asked, "Now do you have anything to say?"

He said, "Yes, would you please tell my son to come take my place in China?"

Well, we've heard these kinds of stories from all lands and ages. The blood of the martyrs has flowed, from Abel to this present time. And in this book on how Jesus treated people, we would be remiss if we didn't consider how He related to His followers—not only in fellowship but in suffering as well.

Christ told His followers, "Be thou faithful unto death, and I will give thee a crown of life." Revelation 2:10. The apostle Peter learned the value of suffering. There was a time when he drew back. You may recall his conversation with Jesus, when Jesus had been telling the disciples about His approaching death. Peter said, "Be it far from thee, Lord." And Jesus rebuked him. See Matthew 16:22, 23.

But Peter learned the blessing of fellowship in suffering, and in 1 Peter 4:12, 13, he said, "Beloved, think it not strange concerning the fiery trial which is to try you. As though some strange thing happened unto you: but rejoice, inasmuch as ye are partakers of Christ's sufferings; that, when his glory shall be revealed, ye may be glad also with exceeding joy."

So it's not strange when Christians suffer. You find a similar message from the apostle Paul in Philippians 1:29, where he wrote, "For unto you it is given in the behalf of Christ, not only to believe on him, but also to suffer for his sake."

It is a privilege and a gift and an honor—one of the greatest blessings that heaven can bestow—to know the fellowship of suffering and to be faithful unto death. It is a mystery to the human mind why this is true, but fellowship in suffering is what Jesus offers to all of His followers in one way or another.

For that reason, let's focus on one of Jesus' closest followers, of whom Jesus Himself said, "None greater has been born." His name was John the Baptist. Many have wondered at his death.

John the Baptist was a miracle child, dedicated to the Lord from birth. He spent his time in the desert, wearing strange garments and eating carob pods and wild honey. He learned to love the desert and the wide-open spaces.

When his public ministry began, announcing the soon-to-come Messiah, he didn't spare any words. He even rebuked King Herod about his marriage. Herod's wife didn't like what he said, so she convinced her husband to throw John the Baptist into prison.

Most people expected John to be released before long. They were sure that the regard of the people and even of King Herod himself would insure John's safety. But John the Baptist waited and waited and waited. The confines of the dungeon weighed heavily on him whose life had been spent in the desert mountains. Questions began to come to his mind. He was given opportunity to doubt his mission—to doubt the divinity of Christ.

The time came when he could bear it no longer, and he sent a message to Jesus, asking some of his hard questions. And the response of Jesus reassured him.

Then one day Herod's wife got her wish. She tricked her husband, through her daughter Salome, and in the process John the Baptist was beheaded—apparently forsaken by God, apparently forgotten by Jesus, apparently left alone. Is that how Jesus treats His disciples?

It is hard for us to understand that of all the gifts heaven can bestow, fellowship with Christ in His sufferings is the most weighty trust and the highest honor. What kind of fellowship did John the Baptist and the missionary in China and all the other martyrs through the ages have with Christ in His sufferings? What are Christ's sufferings?

In the first place, we know that Christ suffered because of righteousness. It was *not* suffering on account of His sin. And He pronounced a blessing on those in all ages who have suffered for righteousness' sake.

The unrighteous have always been uncomfortable in the presence of the righteous. Evil men hated Jesus for His life of purity and tried to destroy Him for that reason. Those who have accepted Christ's righteousness are warned that they will not always be the most popular, and some will suffer persecution and even death for righteousness' sake.

Jesus also suffered for the sake of others. He is the supreme example of One who was willing to lay down His life for His friends, and others in all ages have joined Him in that. We have heard their stories.

We also know that Jesus suffered because He was surrendered to the master plan, formed before the foundation of the world, that if sin should enter, He would come to offer an escape to mankind. Jesus did not deviate from that plan, but remained under His Father's control throughout His entire lifetime on this earth.

But He *could* have saved Himself. When the priests and scribes came by and said, "He saved others; himself he cannot save" (Mark 15:31), they were telling the truth. But although He could have saved Himself, He couldn't save Himself and others too.

Those who have followed Jesus in fellowship have discovered

the same thing. In remaining under the control of God, they haven't been able to save themselves. The missionary in China apparently could have saved himself, had he been willing to deny his faith in Christ. But because he was determined to remain under God's control and to continue confessing his faith in Christ, he could *not* save himself.

So a follower of Christ can suffer for righteousness' sake, he can suffer for the sake of others, and he can suffer because he remains under God's control. John the Baptist experienced this suffering.

Gladly would Jesus have delivered His beloved and faithful servant, but for the sake of the thousands who in later years would pass from prison to death, John was to drink the cup of martyrdom.

John the Baptist blazed the trail for the other disciples, all but one of whom would die a martyr's death. And the disciples paid the ultimate price, blazing the trail for the martyrs who followed them. And the martyrs who followed blazed the trail for us today, who are still living in a world of pain and heartache and separation and death.

We can perhaps understand John's dying for the sake of the martyrs to come—but why did the martyrs have to die?

We know to begin with that God designed His world so that the rain falls on the just and on the unjust. The sun shines on the good and on the bad. If good things happened only to the good and bad things only to the bad, it wouldn't be long before a world full of people would be serving God only for what they could get out of Him. But God wants only the service of love. He has never promised His followers "skies always blue." He has not promised release from the troubles that come from living in this world of sin.

There are undoubtedly many reasons for this. One might be that even for those who are followers of Christ, there is need to be reminded of the awfulness of sin, lest we forget its deadly nature and once again fall victim to it. In God's plan, once the entire universe is clean, once sin and sinners are no more, He wants it to stay that way. He has promised that sin will never rise up the second time. And in order for that to happen, we have to see it clearly for what it is, so that it will never again be appealing to us.

But there is another reason we should consider. We know that the devil has constantly charged God with being unfair. He claims that people serve God only for what they can get out of Him. You know the story of Job and how that turned out. The devil's charge was, Job serves You because of the way You bless him. See Job 1:9, 10. And the experience of Job can be repeated in the lives of each of us living today.

The promise of God is that there is nothing the devil can do, no trouble he can cause in this world of sin, but that God has the power to bring us through, still trusting in Him. And God needs real-life exhibits that this is true.

Let's get more specific as we try to see how this principle works in the great controversy between Christ and Satan. The Bible teaches that at the end of the 1,000 years, when Jesus comes back to this world for the third time, everyone who has ever lived will meet for the first and last time. There will be some on the outside of the city, looking in—and there will be some on the inside of the city, looking out.

On the outside of the city will be some from the days of the Flood, when the thoughts of men's hearts were only evil continually. And they will shake their fists at God and say, "It's not fair. It was too hard to serve You in the time in which I lived."

And perhaps you can imagine a voice from somewhere inside the city, that says, "Noah, will you please step up on the wall?"

And as Noah stands up, the people from the days of the Flood will have nothing more to say.

I can see a group outside the city on that day who lived at the time of Israel's apostasy. And they gave in to the pressure and became worshipers of Baal. They shake their fists at God and say, "It was too hard to serve You when I was living on the earth. Why, I would have been almost the only one who did."

And God asks Elijah to stand up on the wall, and they have nothing more to say.

I can see people from the early church, when persecution was at its height, who are on the outside of the wall and who shake their fists at God and say, "It was too hard to serve You in my time. They were going to kill me if I spoke out boldly for Jesus Christ."

And God sends Stephen to the wall, and they have nothing more to say.

I see a group from the Middle Ages who are shaking their fists at God, and Huss and Jerome are asked to stand up. I see someone from China, from the days of the Boxer Rebellion, on the outside of the wall, and the missionary we noticed earlier is called forth.

I see someone in our day— a victim of cancer who suffers for months and finally dies. And before he dies he becomes angry with God and blames Him for all of his troubles and curses God and dies.

For someone like that, on the outside of the city someday, God may need to have one on the inside who suffered a similar trial, but who still loved and trusted Him regardless.

Well, does this mean that God is the One who brings all this suffering? No, no. Suffering is inflicted by Satan, but is over-ruled by God for purposes of mercy. The disciples asked Jesus, "Who sinned—this man or his parents?"

Jesus said, "Neither—but watch! Now you will see the glory of God." See John 9:3.

A day will come when the glory of God will triumph and the followers of Christ who have suffered and have served Him for His sake—not just for their own—will have their reward. Jesus has promised to more than make it up to us for any inconvenience we suffer as a result of being born here in this world of sin.

And God's plan in the great controversy is proceeding in such a way that even those on the outside of the city—even Satan himself—will finally admit that God has been fair and just.

What a day that will be, when the problem of sin is forever settled and we can be with Christ in fellowship forever!

How Jesus Treated His Neighbors

The word traveled quickly from one to another that Jesus was coming to town. Not that He had been away from town for that long. For almost thirty years He had been just one of the neighbors there in Nazareth. It was less than two years now since He had packed up His tools, said good-bye to His mother Mary, and left on a strange mission.

Reports had filtered back from the river Jordan, from the capital city of Jerusalem, and from other towns and villages in Galilee. Jesus had been doing mysterious things. Often by the village well or in the marketplace, the men and women in Nazareth discussed the latest rumors about Jesus. Most of the stories sounded quite out of character with the Jesus they had known. There in the town of Nazareth Jesus had been a hard worker, a kind listener, a good neighbor. He had been somewhat eccentric, intensely interested in the things of God and going out of His way to be helpful to those around Him. But now suddenly He sounded like some sort of fanatic, radical, or zealot.

He hadn't been gone very long before the townspeople heard about His cleansing of the temple at Jerusalem. He had never tried anything like that at the local synagogue in Nazareth! But after all, maybe Jerusalem *needed* that kind of treatment. Things were pretty corrupt there at the nation's headquarters—or so it was said.

Jesus had traveled quite a bit about the countryside, and a growing number followed Him wherever He went. Reports increased of miracles, healings, and exorcisms. No one knew for sure what to believe, but all were interested in learning about the Hometown Boy making good—or was the Hometown Boy making trouble? Well, now they'd find out for themselves, for Jesus was coming back to Nazareth for a visit.

"Jesus returned in the power of the Spirit into Galilee: and there went out a fame of him through all the region round about. And he taught in their synagogues, being glorified of all. And he came to Nazareth, where he had been brought up: and, as his custom was, he went into the synagogue on the sabbath day, and stood up for to read." Luke 4:14-16.

The people of Nazareth watched with fond pride as Jesus was given the honor of reading the scripture that Sabbath morning. It was nice to have Him home again. It was nice of the local elders to give Him the privilege of being on the platform. Can't you hear someone whispering to his neighbor, "This is Joseph's son, you know. He used to live just down the street from us."

John the Baptist had proclaimed Jesus to be the Son of God. His disciples believed Him to be the Messiah. Multitudes had accepted Him as a great teacher or prophet. But here in Nazareth, He was the son of Joseph. And if there *was* anything to the reports of the miracles and wonders He had performed in other places, wasn't Nazareth entitled to a special show? Didn't they have a right to the front-row seats? Hadn't they "known Him when"? They leaned forward to catch His words.

"And there was delivered unto him the book of the prophet Esaias. And when he had opened the book, he found the place where it was written, The Spirit of the Lord is upon me, because he hath anointed me to preach the gospel to the poor; he hath sent me to heal the brokenhearted, to preach deliverance to the captives, and recovering of sight to the blind, to set at liberty them that are bruised, to preach the acceptable year of the Lord. And he closed the book, and he gave it again to the minister, and sat down. And the eyes of all them that were in the synagogue were fastened on him." Luke 4:17-20.

Perhaps most of the people of Nazareth missed the emphasis. They knew this particular passage of Scripture was a Messianic statement, and they thought of the Messiah to come. Per-

haps a few were beginning already to put two and two together—and to be uncomfortable. But for all of them, something in the air prevented the service from continuing, for the
Bible says the eyes of all were fastened on Him, even after He
sat down.

Then Jesus spoke again, in verse 21: "And he began to say
unto them, This day is this scripture fulfilled in your ears." And
now the rest of the faces grew dark. Jesus was essentially saying, "I am the Messiah." Pretty hard words to accept when
spoken about your next-door neighbor. But there was something even harder to accept. If Jesus was saying, "I am the
Messiah," He was *also* saying, "You people are poor. You people
are captives. You people are blind and in prison."

What a way for Jesus to treat His neighbors! Didn't they deserve His respect and honor? Hadn't they treated Him politely?
What a way to respond! Why—if He wanted them to believe in
Him—didn't He begin by healing the diseases and afflictions of
all of His old friends and neighbors? Why—if He was the
Messiah—didn't He begin by offering them key positions in His
new kingdom they had heard about? How could He begin by
insulting them and then go on to expect their support and acceptance?

In spite of the interest in Jesus as the Hometown Boy who
had made it big in Jerusalem and Capernaum, in spite of the
gracious words He spoke, in spite of the strong influence of the
Holy Spirit present that day, the seeds of rejection were strong.
The people said, "Is not this Joseph's son?" Verse 22.

What were they saying? They were saying, "He's one of us."
Go ahead, Jesus, strike out against the corruption at Jerusalem. Let everybody know about the sinfulness of the heathen
and the Samaritans. Rebuke the harlots and tax collectors. But
this is Nazareth! Don't treat your neighbors like this! You're
one of us. We helped make you what you are. Don't put on airs
with us—we *know* you. We know your parents and family. We
know you're just the son of Joseph.

But Jesus wasn't finished yet. "And he said unto them, Ye
will surely say unto me this proverb, Physician, heal thyself:
whatsoever we have heard done in Capernaum, do also here in

thy country." Verse 23. And He proceeded to remind them of the time of Elijah, when there was no rain for three and a half years and, in spite of the many widows in Israel, Elijah was sent to a widow in Sarepta, a city of Sidon—to an outsider. God had passed by His people of that day and had gone to the heathen. Not only that, Jesus reminded them of Naaman the leper, who was healed by Elisha, while none of the lepers in Israel were healed. And now Jesus was suggesting that the same thing would happen again in Nazareth. It was too much to take.

"And all they in the synagogue, when they heard these things, were filled with wrath." Verse 28. *All* of them!

Wait a minute—these were people Jesus had grown up with. These were people who had played games with Him in the streets—when they were playing games that Jesus would play. These people has seen Him as a boy, leaving the village of Nazareth in the early morning or evening hours with a scroll under His arm, going out into the hills for a quiet time with His Father. These were people who had seen His perfect life, who had been given a cup of cold water by His hands, who had shared His lunch when they were hungry. Mark tells us that His own family was there as well, though we would surely want to hope their reaction was the exception. But it says *all* of them were filled with wrath.

They "rose up, and thrust him out of the city, and led him unto the brow of the hill whereon their city was built, that they might cast him down headlong. But he passing through the midst of them went his way." Verses 29, 30.

Can you see Him walking away from Nazareth, alone? Can you see His bowed head, the tears on His face? These were His friends from earliest childhood. Surely He loved these people in a special way. But they had rejected Him—and not only that, they had tried to kill Him! Another heartbreak had come to this Man of Sorrows who was acquainted with grief. His own neighbors and friends, and even perhaps some of His own family members, had rejected Him.

What was the basis of their rejection? It went much deeper than the rivalry of His own townspeople and neighbors. They rejected Him because He was pure and they were sinful. The ungodly have always been uncomfortable in the presence of the godly. They rejected Him because they knew they would have to accept change if they accepted His teachings. They rejected Him because their national pride had been dealt a heavy blow. They did not wish to consider the Old Testament account of times when heathen and outsiders had been honored above the chosen people. They rejected Him because He did not give proper respect to their religious lives, to their religious customs, or even to their religious leaders whom they revered. They rejected Jesus because He was like them—and yet He was not like them.

So Jesus was forced to walk away from His neighbors at Nazareth and to disappear down the dusty road with the tragic realization that for most of them, the rejection was final. He knew that once people have rejected God, to continue rejecting Him is almost inevitable. Human pride resists ever admitting that it has been in the wrong. When we've once taken a position, we don't like to back down. And for most of the neighbors of Jesus, this rejection at Nazareth was never reversed.

Yet even in Nazareth, there were a few. Mark 6 indicates that He was able to heal a few. In the chosen nation, from among God's special people, there were a few. There have always been a few who accept, and I desperately want to be among those who accept Him today, don't you?

Jesus came to preach the gospel to the poor. There were a few poor fishermen who accepted Him. Wouldn't you like to join them today? Jesus came to heal the brokenhearted. There were a few brokenhearted ones, like Mary and Martha, who learned to sit at His feet. Jesus came to preach deliverance to the captives. There were a few who heard the words of Jesus above the roar of demons in their darkened minds and accepted the deliverance He offered. Jesus came to give sight to the blind. And there were a few, like blind Bartimaeus, who cried out for the help He longed to give. There were a few of the spiritually blind who sensed their need—who reached out for Jesus and whose sight was restored as well. There were a few who had been beaten and bruised by the enemy, who came to Jesus and accepted His deliverance and shouted His praises.

But there were only a few.

As you see Jesus going down the road, forced away from those who have rejected His love, don't let Him go alone. Don't let Him go alone today, but walk beside Him and say, "Dear Lord, count me in. I'm on Your side. I don't want to turn You down."

He is still looking with great longing for the few who will accept the blessings He is waiting to bestow.

How Jesus Treated the Religious Leaders

Are you a Pharisee? Or are you a Sadducee? If you have had even a little exposure to the Bible account of the life of Christ, you would probably not want to be identified with either group! But in the days of Christ, to be a Pharisee or Sadducee was a mark of distinction. Even the apostle Paul spoke of being a Pharisee as honorable. In those days, if you met up with an old friend who asked, "What is your son doing now?" you were proud to say, "My son is a Pharisee!"

But today we think of Pharisees and Sadducees largely in negative terms, even though some of the problems they had may be problems we find in our own hearts. Let's look at what made these people tick, and perhaps we will see how we can be saved from the mistakes they made.

Who were the Pharisees? They were the conservatives. They were rigid legalists. They were traditionalists. They went to a great deal of trouble to uphold the standards and doctrines and practices of the church. They were victims of the common problem of those days—salvation by works. They were trying to save themselves by their own efforts. They were the larger of the two groups of religious leaders and found their security in the standards of the church which they upheld.

The second group of church leaders were the Sadducees. They were the liberals of the days of Jesus. They were still legalists, because they were equally victims of the idea that you can save yourself by your own efforts. But they found their security in the standards of the church which they abandoned.

The Sadducees claimed to believe in "sola scriptura," as opposed to the Pharisees, who openly supported some of their doctrines by tradition. But in fact, the Sadducees had their own traditions as well. And even in their emphasis on the Scriptures, they were often very selective as to which to accept and which to leave out.

Among the Sadducees were Jesus' worst enemies. They were the smaller of the two groups but the more powerful. The position of high priest was usually awarded to a Sadducee, and they controlled the Sanhedrin.

In surveys taken in the Christian church today, it has been shown that the majority of religious leaders and people alike are still trying to get to heaven by their own works. This permeates all Christian churches. It has long been the common denominator of all world religions, but it has become common to the Christian faith as well.

Every church struggles with the disease known as salvation by works. The majority of so-called Christians have no time for God, no time for prayer, no time for the study of His Word. And anyone living life apart from God day by day, yet hoping for heaven at last, is a believer in salvation by works. Which means that we have a high possibility that Pharisees and Sadducees are among us today.

The Pharisees and Sadducees had other things in common in addition to the hope for salvation on the basis of their own efforts. They had a common problem of misinterpreting Scripture. They misinterpreted the law and its purpose and function. They misinterpreted prophecy, including the prophecies of the Messiah to come. They misunderstood the kingdom of God and what was involved in the good news of His kingdom. Yet they were great on justification! The blood ran like rivers at their feasts and religious festivals. They were daily involved in the sacrifices of lambs and cattle and doves. But in spite of their common beliefs and interests, little unity existed between the two groups. They were constantly involved in controversy and debate. Often their arguments were over the resurrection of the dead.

When Jesus came along, He didn't treat them very well, according to their standards. He not only didn't honor them and their forms and ceremonies, but He was actually insulting! It's hard to understand how He could have spoken to them as He did and still have tears in His voice, but that's the way we are told He was. In Luke 12:1, He called both the Pharisees and Sadducees hypocrites. They were both wrong. They were both trying to appear something different on the outside from what they really were on the inside. In Matthew 23 Jesus used an interesting illustration of their problem, talking about the cup and saucer which were clean on the outside but still unclean on the inside.

Even more severe was His illustration about the tombs of the prophets, in Matthew 23, verses 27-30. He said, "Woe unto you, scribes and Pharisees, hypocrites! for ye are like unto whited sepulchres, which indeed appear beautiful outward, but are within full of dead men's bones, and of all uncleanness. Even so ye also outwardly appear righteous unto men, but within ye are full of hypocrisy and iniquity. Woe unto you, scribes and Pharisees, hypocrites! because ye build the tombs of the prophets, and garnish the sepulchres of the righteous, and say, If we had been in the days of our fathers, we would not have been partakers with them in the blood of the prophets."

Obviously they were victims of external righteousness. They knew how to beat a path from their homes to the church or synagogue. But Jesus said, in His Sermon on the Mount, that unless your righteousness exceeds the righteousness of the Pharisees, there's no chance for the kingdom of heaven.

These hypocrites were tithe payers, they were rigid Sabbath keepers, they were health reformers. They wouldn't even eat a gnat in the soup. They were good on works—especially the works that could be seen by others. They were great on fasting and could pray long prayers. They were meticulous about their ceremonial washings and loved the first place in the synagogue. But they brought to others burdens impossible to lift, and Jesus said to them that when they succeeded in cramming their religion down someone else's throat, they made their convert "twofold more the child of hell than yourselves." Matthew 23:15.

Jesus said, "I, if I be lifted up from the earth, will draw all men unto me." John 12:32. But the religious leaders said, "If we draw all unto us, then we will be lifted up." And that is precisely what they tried to do.

These religious leaders didn't like Jesus for a number of reasons. First, Jesus received sinners, and they didn't. Sinning sinners didn't stand a chance with the Pharisees and Sadducees. They put them out of the synagogue, they tried to stone them, and they would not associate with them. But Jesus received sinners—and that's good news even today, isn't it? Aren't you glad that Jesus receives sinners?

Another thing they didn't like about Jesus was that, according to their rules, He broke the Sabbath. They considered Him a liberal, because He didn't follow their rules and traditions. They didn't like the way Jesus went about teaching without the proper authorization. They didn't like the lack of respect He gave their high office. They didn't like the names He called them and the unsparing rebukes He directed their way. They didn't like His miracle working and the way the common people flocked after Him and shouted His praises. They said, "The whole world is gone after him." John 12:19. And they feared for their own power and authority over the people.

In short, they were envious and covetous, and when the lonely cross arose as a result of their determined hatred of Christ, they came by and wagged their heads and said, "He saved others; Himself He cannot save." They had spent their lifetimes trying to save themselves, and the fact that Jesus came not to save Himself but to save others was a slap in the face. Jesus could have saved Himself, but that's not why He came. He came to save others, including you and me, and so long as He did that, He could not save Himself as well.

Self-surrender was the essence of Jesus' teachings, and this was particularly offensive to the religious leaders. They were big enough to handle their own lives. They could do it themselves. Especially were the Sadducees offended, for they did not believe in a God who was personally involved in the lives of His children. So they were offended by the teaching and example of Jesus Christ.

Paul speaks of these religious leaders in 1 Corinthians 2:7, 8. "We speak the wisdom of God in a mystery, even the hidden wisdom, which God ordained before the world unto our glory: which none of the princes of this world knew: for had they known it, they would not have crucified the Lord of glory." Jesus suggested the same thought in His prayer at the crucifixion—"Father, forgive them; for they know not what they do." Luke 23:34. Apparently there was some ignorance involved, and had they known He was the Son of God, they wouldn't have crucified Him.

But *why* didn't they know? The shepherds knew, and the wise men from the East knew. The humble fishermen knew, and even the devils knew and said, we "know thee who thou art." But not the religious leaders. Perhaps we can find a clue as to why they didn't know in Matthew 11:25: "At that time Jesus answered and said, I thank thee, O Father, Lord of heaven and earth, because thou hast hid these things from the wise and prudent, and hast revealed them unto babes."

Jesus was thankful that these things were hidden from the wise. Why? What do wise people do with truth? They take the glory to themselves. The tendency is to take glory to ourselves if we can find the slightest excuse for doing so.

Did God sit up there on His throne and say, "Give it to the fishermen and the shepherds, but don't let the Pharisees have any truth?" Or do we have further Scripture to examine on this point? Look at Matthew 13, beginning with verse 9: "Who hath ears to hear, let him hear. And the disciples came, and said unto him, Why speakest thou unto them in parables? He answered and said unto them, Because it is given unto you to know the mysteries of the kingdom of heaven, but to them it is not given." Don't stop there—read on! "For whosoever hath, to him shall be given, and he shall have more abundance: but whosoever hath not, from him shall be taken away even that he hath. Therefore speak I to them in parables: because they seeing see not; and hearing they hear not, neither do they understand. And in them is fulfilled the prophecy of Esaias, which saith, By hearing ye shall hear, and shall not understand; and seeing ye shall see, and shall not perceive: for this people's heart is waxed gross, and their ears are dull of hearing, and their eyes they have closed; lest at any time they should see with their eyes, and hear with their ears, and should understand with their heart, and should be converted, and I should heal them. But blessed are your eyes, for they see: and your ears, for they hear." Verses 9-16. Their ears *they* have closed. Their eyes *they* have closed.

So then it wasn't God who arbitrarily gave understanding to some and not to others. It was the difference in the people. The sun shines on the wax, and the sun shines on the clay. The wax softens; the clay hardens. Why? It's the same sun shining on both.

Why did they close their eyes and ears? Jesus, coming the way He did, threatened their pride of status. He bypassed the religious leaders and chose the peasants and foreigners to deliver His message. Pride of status had been threatened.

Second, their national pride had been dealt a low blow. They had expected a Messiah to come at the head of armies and vanquish Rome. Instead, He came in humble guise and offered His gifts to Jews and Gentiles alike.

And third, their personal pride was threatened. The sinners and the harlots and the thieves accepted Jesus, and He accepted them. How could this be, when the religious rulers felt nothing but uncomfortable in His presence? So they closed their eyes and set their course away from Him. And just like the people of Nazareth, once they had taken this stand, they were too proud to change their position.

In spite of their differences, the Pharisees and Sadducees finally got together. They could have found unity in the acceptance of Jesus had they been willing to surrender their pride and come to Him, for it is in coming to Jesus that we are drawn close to one another. But instead they got together in their rejection of Him and met in unity in the judgment hall of Pilate and at the crucifixion.

What if you see yourself when you look at these religious leaders from the days of Christ? Does this mean your case is hopeless? No, there is good news, for you can join with those who were the exception to the rule.

Nicodemus, a Pharisee and a member of the Sanhedrin, was too proud even to approach Jesus by day, but instead sought Him under cover of darkness. Yet he accepted the new birth Jesus so solemnly emphasized and became a faithful follower in the end.

Simon, also a Pharisee, took the long route to Jesus. Even being healed of his leprosy was not enough to turn him around, yet the time came when Jesus was able to reach his heart—at his own feast—and Simon surrendered to the love that would not let him go.

And John 12:42, 43 speaks of "many" who believed in Him. There were many who learned the futility of their own efforts to save themselves and came to accept the salvation Jesus had to offer. They recognized that they could not cleanse the temple of their own hearts, and they invited Jesus to come in, not once only, but day by day. Jesus is still offering the same salvation to each one of us, and we can choose to accept. We can choose to enter into a vital relationship with Him as we learn to know Him better as Saviour, Lord, and Friend.

How Jesus Treated the Common People

Did you ever play the game of follow-the-leader when you were small? And as you played the game, did you ever find yourself going into the swimming pool with all your clothes on, wading through mud puddles, or jumping off the garage roof? If so, you probably learned to seriously question the game!

Sheep are notorious for following the leader. In a slaughterhouse in New York City, they had trained a goat to be the leader. His name was Judas. He would go through the gate as soon as it opened, and all the sheep would follow him blindly. At the last minute, the goat slipped out through a little side gate, and the sheep continued to their fate while the goat went back for another load.

One of the shortest parables spoken by Jesus is on the subject of the dangers of playing follow-the-leader in a spiritual sense. It's found in Luke 6:39, 40. "And he spake a parable unto them, Can the blind lead the blind? shall they not both fall into the ditch? The disciple is not above his master: but every one that is perfect shall be as his master."

Jesus often compares His followers to sheep, and we are invited to follow where He leads. So the problem is not with the following, but with who it is that is leading you. In the days of Christ, the Pharisees and Sadducees were accepted as leaders by the vast majority of the common people. As we noticed in the last chapter, the Pharisees were the traditionalists, the conservatives; and the Sadducees were the liberals. Both groups were legalists, because both groups depended on their own efforts to secure salvation. And the people lined up behind their leaders—their *blind* leaders—and joined them in rejecting Jesus in the end.

It is a tragic fact that people seldom rise higher than their minister or teacher or leader. The Jewish people perished as a nation because they followed their leaders into error. They did not search the Scriptures for themselves and did not decide for themselves what was truth. And is not this a great danger for us today? How easy it is simply to follow, rather than to study and search and pray for ourselves to know the voice of the true Shepherd.

Another similar text concerning following leaders is found in Matthew 15:13, 14. This came right after Jesus had said some hard things to the religious leaders of that day. And His disciples asked Him, Did You know that the Pharisees were offended when they heard what You said? And then Jesus "answered and said, Every plant, which my heavenly Father hath not planted, shall be rooted up. Let them alone: they be blind leaders of the blind. And if the blind lead the blind, both shall fall into the ditch." Apparently it is possible to find leaders even in a religious community who are not planted by the Lord. Not all who are outwardly members of the body of Christ are trees of righteousness. And the time will come when those who are not planted by the Lord will be uprooted.

I would like to make a disclaimer at this point. When we talk about following the leaders today, we are not speaking just of Washington, D.C. The practice of following the leader is not limited to the church headquarters. This is by no means taking potshots at Washington. People pick their own leaders—depending on how they wish to live. And you can always find someone, somewhere, who will lead you in the direction you want to go. God has ordained leadership as a means of guiding in His work and His church. Leadership has a valid purpose and function. The point here is that it is dangerous to follow *anyone* blindly.

According to available surveys and statistics, only one out of four or five in the church today is spending any time at all in personal fellowship and study of God's Word. If that is the case, then we have a lot of blind followers today as well. So let's not just look at this as a history lesson but see where we can profit by the lessons Jesus tried to teach the rank and file of His day.

So it was in this setting that Jesus gave the parable teaching that it is possible to follow a leader right into the ditch. Why was this so? What was the trouble with the common people, the crowds that followed, that made them so easily deceived?

First, they were not converted. They had never experienced the supernatural work of the Holy Spirit on the human heart. Their attitude toward God had not been changed. They had never allowed God to give them a new capacity for knowing Him that they did not possess. They spent little time in personally seeking God because the capacity wasn't even there. In the days of Christ, they tied bits of Scripture around their wrists and heads as a substitute for hiding it in their hearts. All of their religious activity focused on self. They were comfortable with an external religion and accepted the forms and ceremonies, but their hearts were untouched by the grace of God.

These people had no relationship with God. They were victims of salvation by works, and their motive in their religious exercises and standards was to secure temporal blessings. They liked the idea of the grasshoppers stopping at the fence line of the one who paid his tithe. They were interested in heaven and the offer of living forever. They were impressed by the loaves and the fishes—and the diseases that were banished by a few quiet words from Jesus. But in John 6, when Jesus spoke of the bread of life, they were troubled and said, "This is an hard saying; who can hear it?" Verse 60.

The people in the days of Jesus gave Him only a limited acceptance. They were willing to accept Him as a great Teacher. They were willing to accept Him as a worker of miracles. They were willing to believe He was a prophet. But they refused to accept Him as Saviour or Lord or God. And their limited acceptance ended in total rejection.

The people then had problems with accepting the spirit of prophecy. You find this in Luke 16:19-31, where Jesus uses a well-known Roman fable to teach several truths—the condition of mankind after death NOT being one of them! But the rich man, as you recall, was in torment. And he asked that Lazarus, the beggar, be sent to speak to his five brothers and warn them from the same fate.

"Abraham saith unto him, They have Moses and the prophets; let them hear them. And he said, Nay, father Abraham: but if one went unto them from the dead, they will repent. And he said unto him, If they hear not Moses and the prophets, neither will they be persuaded, though one rose from the dead." Verses 29-31.

Not long afterward one *was* raised from the dead—and his name was Lazarus! Not only did they refuse to accept that evidence, they plotted to kill both Jesus and Lazarus whom He had raised. So these people had a hard time with Moses and the prophets.

Matthew 23 says they garnished the tombs of the prophets, yet they were the children of those who had killed the prophets, in spirit as well as in lineage. Paul speaks about this in Acts 13:26, 27. Here Paul is preaching, and he says, "Men and brethren, children of the stock of Abraham. . . . They that dwell at Jerusalem, and their rulers, because they knew him not, nor yet the voices of the prophets which are read every sabbath day, they have fulfilled them in condemning him." They read every Sabbath from the writings of the prophets, but they did not accept or understand what was read.

Stephen said this in Acts 7:51-53: "Ye stiffnecked and uncircumcised in heart and ears, ye do always resist the Holy Ghost: as your fathers did, so do ye. Which of the prophets have not your fathers persecuted? and they have slain them which shewed before of the coming of the Just One; of whom ye have been now the betrayers and murderers: who have received the law by the disposition of angels, and have not kept it."

That was too much for the people there, and they rushed at Stephen, dragged him out of the city, and a young man named Saul stood and collected the coats as the stones began to fly. But Stephen, looking up toward heaven, saw a vision of Jesus, *standing* at the Father's right hand. I've always liked the story. Jesus wasn't going to take this sitting down! He was standing, on Stephen's side, and Stephen died in peace, praying for his enemies. But he had spoken the truth about these people. They professed to accept and revere the prophets, but in reality they rejected both the prophets and the One foretold by the prophets.

This is also evidenced in their relationship to John the Baptist. In Matthew 21, the religious leaders found themselves in a hard place, because Jesus had questioned them as to how they regarded John the Baptist. And they refused to answer, because they knew that the people believed John to be a prophet. But they gave John the Baptist only a limited acceptance, for they did not accept Jesus as the One to whom John the Baptist had pointed.

Did Jesus try to tell the common people that they did not need leaders? No. There is a purpose for leadership. But is the purpose of leadership to hand truth to people without asking any further investigation on their part? Never! The purpose of leaders and teachers and preachers is to encourage and motivate people to understand truth by searching it out for themselves. An old adage says, "You can give a man a fish, and feed him for a day. You can teach a man to fish, and feed him for a lifetime." I don't know if you could call that a vegetarian illustration, but it's a good one nonetheless!

Did Paul teach truth? He certainly did. Did Jesus teach truth? He did. Did His disciples teach truth? Yes, and the Bereans checked it out to see whether it *was* truth—and were commended for their insight. Jesus did not ask the masses to follow Him blindly. He asks no one to follow blindly. But He did ask for them to follow Him.

The majority of the common people in the days of Christ did not accept. But there were exceptions, and they give us courage and inspiration today.

Not all of those among the masses were fickle. Not all joined those who sang His praises at the triumphal entry and then cried, "Crucify Him!" a few days later. The woman at the well was seeking for something to satisfy her soul. She accepted Jesus as Messiah and convinced a whole town of His worth. Lazarus, a workaday man not distinguished at the synagogue, from the time of his first meeting with Jesus loved Him with a love that never waned. The thief on the cross turned his head amidst the pain and shame and cried, "Lord, remember me!" I'm glad for the exceptions, aren't you?

We can join the exceptions today, as did the disciples at the end of Jesus' discourse in John 6. The crowds were leaving, and Jesus asked, Are you going to leave too? See verse 67.

Don't you want to join the disciples as they say, "Lord, to whom shall we go? We believe that you are the Christ, the Son of the Living God." See verse 68. Believing in Jesus was not popular. It was not the "in" thing with the crowd to continue following Jesus when He was here—and it still isn't. But I would like to invite you to a twofold experience that will keep you from blindly following anyone and being misled. First, a relationship with Jesus for yourself. Second, an intelligent understanding of the truth on which that relationship is based. Those two are equally important. One without the other is not going to do it. But we can accept today the privilege of knowing Jesus and knowing truth for ourselves, as we seek Him in His Word and through prayer. And we can continue to seek Him until He comes again.

How Jesus Treated the Non-Church Members

A whole carload of students were riding home from college one time for spring vacation. As we rode along, we passed a sign that said, "Don't read the other side of this sign!" Nobody said anything, but as we passed, every head in the car turned to read the back of the sign! Negative publicity can be a very effective form of advertising. Maybe even God can use it on occasion.

As Jesus came to the close of His life and mission here in this world, things didn't look very good. There was a lot of bad press—bad publicity. Many people were forsaking Him, even from among those He had healed. Nine out of ten lepers accepted only the physical blessings, while refusing the offer of spiritual blessing.

For a while the crowds had flocked to hear and see Him. But as His time here on earth neared an end, His whole mission had the appearance of cruel defeat. The case seemed hopeless. Jesus had apparently done little of the work He had come to do.

Yet in spite of apparent failure, He could sit on the top of Mount Olivet, look across to another mountain that looked like a skull, and say, This gospel that I teach will go to all the world. As far as human resources were concerned, there wasn't a ghost of a chance. He had only a few disciples and a handful of women as His followers—and even His disciples took off on a hundred-yard dash when the crucial moment came. It seemed apparent to everyone that He would never be accepted by the church leaders. Success looked impossible.

But we have lived to see the fulfillment of His prediction—or at least the potential in our own day for its fulfillment. Today the church too is getting a lot of bad publicity. But God can also turn this around, even as the dismal prospects were turned around in the days of Jesus' first advent. Bad publicity is still publicity. Being told not to read the other side of the sign can cause people to read the other side of the sign. So there are lessons to be learned today from the apparent failure marking the days just prior to the crucifixion of Jesus.

Let's begin by reading John 12:20 and onward, where an episode is recorded that brought courage to the heart of Christ. "And there were certain Greeks among them that came up to worship at the feast." Jesus was present at the feast, standing in the court of the temple—the narthex of the church, if you please—about to turn and leave it for the last time.

They "came therefore to Philip, which was of Bethsaida of Galilee, and desired him, saying, Sir, we would see Jesus. Philip cometh and telleth Andrew: and again Andrew and Philip tell Jesus. And Jesus answered them, saying, The hour is come, that the Son of man should be glorified." John 12: 21-23.

Then begins a paragraph that at first glance may not look too relevant but on second glance becomes very meaningful. "Verily, verily, I say unto you, Except a corn of wheat fall into the ground and die, it abideth alone: but if it die, it bringeth forth much fruit." Verse 24. Jesus was indicating that He was going to be glorified but that He must first die. Then He makes the application to His followers. "He that loveth his life shall lose it; and he that hateth his life in this world shall keep it unto life eternal. If any man serve me [or shall we say, become My servant], let him follow me." Follow where? Jesus was headed for the cross! "And where I am, there shall also my servant be: if any man serve me, him will my Father honour." Verses 25, 26. So Jesus was indicating that in order for us to be glorified, we must follow Him to the cross.

"Now is my soul troubled; and what shall I say? Father, save me from this hour." We understand that as far as Jesus was concerned, if He'd had His preference, He would just as soon not have gone to the cross. But then came His immediate submission to the will of His Father and the plan of salvation: "But for this cause came I unto this hour. Father, glorify thy name.

"Then came there a voice from heaven, saying, I have both glorified it, and will glorify it again. The people therefore, that stood by, and heard it, said that it thundered: others said, An angel spake to him. Jesus answered and said, This voice came not because of me, but for your sakes." Verses 27-30. God gave one more opportunity, one last chance, for them to listen. But notice that God's voice sounds like only thunder to some people. "Now is the judgment of this world: now shall the prince of this world be cast out. And I, if I be lifted up from the earth, will draw all men unto me." Verses 31, 32.

What an encouragement it must have been to the heart of Jesus when these men from the West came and said, We would like to see Jesus. This was one of the few encouraging notes at the end of His life, for He was under the shadow of the cross. He had predicted it, even though His followers didn't like the idea. But the appearance of these men came as a fulfillment to a prophecy recorded in Matthew 8:11, 12. Jesus had just healed the centurion's servant and commended the military leader for his great faith. Then He had made this statement: "Many shall come from the east and west, and shall sit down with Abraham, and Isaac, and Jacob, in the kingdom of heaven. But the children of the kingdom shall be cast out into outer darkness: there shall be weeping and gnashing of teeth."

Jesus predicted a trade, a time in which His own professed people would leave Him—and other people would come from the east and west (and Luke adds, from the north and south as well) and sit down with Abraham and Isaac and Jacob. At the very beginning of Jesus' ministry, the wise men came from the East and asked, "Where is he that is born King of the Jews? for we have seen his star in the east, and are come to worship him." Matthew 2:2. Then, at the end of His ministry a group came from the West—the continuing fulfillment of this prophecy.

Did you notice Philip and Andrew? They had their radar on. Their ears were tuned to the searching soul, and they saw the Greeks who had entered the temple courtyard. Way back at the beginning, it was Andrew who brought his brother Peter to

Jesus. And you can see Andrew sitting on the back row of the synagogue while Peter is up front preaching. And Andrew says to himself, "What a wonderful day it was when I brought Peter to Jesus." Andrew was willing to be on the sidelines. He wasn't always up front and talkative. But he was always bringing someone to Jesus—even if just a boy with five loaves and two small fish.

Philip, one of the first disciples of Jesus, had brought Nathanael, inviting him to "Come and see." So here they are again, Philip and Andrew, bringing someone to Christ.

The Greeks certainly had the right motivation—"We would like to see Jesus." They didn't ask to hear the results of the missionary journey the seventy disciples had been on. They didn't ask for a tour of the synagogue or for a discussion of some theological point. They wanted to see Jesus. And their request was granted.

In this passage of Scripture a classic statement of Jesus is recorded; "I, if I be lifted up . . . , will draw all . . . unto me." The lifting up of Jesus draws people to Him. Jesus lifted up on the cross was an offence to the people of His day—and it is an offence to some in our day as well. The early church had to put up with a lot of negative publicity in having a God who had been crucified. That was bad press. The gods of those days were foreign to the concept of "He saved others; himself he cannot save." Paul spoke in Corinth of the foolishness of preaching the cross. Yet therein was the power of God.

And these Greeks were able to go straight to the heart of the matter, asking for and accepting a revelation of Jesus in a time when others were closing the door of salvation to themselves.

We're told that the church at the end of time, just before Jesus comes again, is going to appear as if about to fall. But it does not fall. Instead, there is to be once again this strange trade—with those inside leaving and those from the north and south and east and west coming in. Notice that Abraham and Isaac and Jacob don't leave the church and go out to join the people from the north and south and east and west. It's the people from the north and south and east and west who come in. Don't miss that!

So you have, in the organic church at the very end, a great exodus of people who have the same problem as the religious people in the days of Christ. They turn Him down. And as these leave, great numbers come in and take their places.

Why does this trade take place? The apostle Paul describes the situation and gives the answer. And if it was good for that day, why not for today?

"What shall we say then? That the Gentiles, which followed not after righteousness, have attained to righteousness, even the righteousness which is of faith. But Israel, which followed after the law of righteousness, hath not attained to the law of righteousness. Wherefore? Because they sought it not by faith, but as it were by the works of the law. For they stumbled at that stumblingstone; as it is written, Behold, I lay in Sion a stumblingstone and rock of offence: and whosoever believeth on him shall not be ashamed.

"Brethren, my heart's desire and prayer to God for Israel is, that they might be saved. For I bear them record that they have a zeal of God, but not according to knowledge. For they being ignorant of God's righteousness [here's the problem], and going to establish their own righteousness, have not submitted themselves unto the righteousness of God." Romans 9:30-33 and 10:1-3.

They hadn't gone to the cross yet and joined Jesus, who would not save Himself. They hadn't come to the place where they realized they could not save themselves. And Paul finishes his argument with these words, "For Christ is the end of the law for righteousness to every one that believeth." Verse 4.

The real issue in salvation by faith and salvation by works is the dividing line between those who accepted Jesus, along with the Greeks, and those who rejected Him, along with the Jewish leaders. People who have achieved through their own efforts want merit and credit, and they find Jesus a stumblingstone and rock of offence. The legalist is offended at Jesus and will leave Him in the end for precisely the same reason.

Can't we join Paul when he says, "Brethren, it is my heart's desire that [how many?]—should be saved." All. We don't want to see thousands from our church go out into darkness, when

God Himself would want every one of us to stay. We can all be there to sit down with Abraham and Isaac and Jacob, along with the multitude that no one can number who come from all nations and kindreds and tongues and people. We cannot save ourselves from being offended, from stumbling at that stumblingstone, except by one method—and that is by falling on the Rock and being broken by our own free choice. We can choose to enter into a relationship with Jesus today, to follow Him and to submit to the truth that we cannot save ourselves. We can join the Greeks by joining with them in seeking to see Jesus today.

"We would see Jesus;" for the shadows lengthen
Across the little landscape of our life;
We would see Jesus, our weak faith to strengthen
For the last conflict, in this mortal strife.

"We would see Jesus;" this is all we're needing—
Strength, joy, and willingness come with the sight;
We would see Jesus, dying, risen, pleading,
Soon to return and end this mortal night!
                                        —Anna B. Warner

How They Treated Jesus in the Garden

When I was a boy in Michigan, we used to ice skate a lot. One night when I was about twelve years old, my preacher father was going across town to give a Bible study. I knew he was going near a park where there was a good ice-skating lake, so I talked him into taking me and dropping me off at the lake while he went on to his Bible study.

They must have been studying about the millennium that night! He was gone for so long that the park closed, everyone else left, the lights went out, and I was alone in the dark, on the lake, trying to skate enough to keep from freezing. After what seemed like an eternity, I finally decided my father had forgotten me and gone home without me. I was too cold to skate anymore, and I just huddled against a tree that gave a little shelter from the wind.

Now twelve-year-old boys don't cry—but they do too! I had all kinds of feelings—feelings bad and sad and mad. But just before I died, I saw the friendly lights of my father's car coming up the road. I was never so overjoyed in my life! But in preparing this chapter I remembered that experience of feeling forsaken by my father.

With this chapter, we make a transition from considering how Jesus treated people to taking a look at how people treated Jesus. We have studied so far many of the groups of people with whom Jesus walked and worked—and how He treated each person with unfailing love and kindness. Now, as we study the closing scenes of His life, we see in tragic display how people responded to His life and mission.

Let's look at the description of how they treated Jesus in the garden. "Then cometh Jesus with them unto a place called Gethsemane, and saith unto the disciples, Sit ye here, while I go and pray yonder. And he took with him Peter and the two sons of Zebedee, and began to be sorrowful and very heavy. Then saith he unto them, My soul is exceeding sorrowful, even unto death." We would probably say, "I feel like I'm going to die."

"Tarry ye here, and watch with me. And he went a little farther, and fell on his face, and prayed, saying, O my Father, if it be possible, let this cup pass from me: nevertheless, not as I will, but as thou wilt." Matthew 26:36-39.

Put the scene together as you recall it. Jesus had spent some time with His disciples in the upper room. They had celebrated the Passover. He had given them some encouraging lessons, some words concerning the vine and the branches, and He had prayed for them with strong prayer—not only in behalf of His disciples (there were only eleven now), but also for His followers of every age.

Together they had left the upper room and started toward the garden, which was one of Jesus' favorite places for prayer and communion with His Father. As they walked along toward the garden, Jesus was overwhelmed with a great burden. The disciples noticed that the heaviness was so great that Jesus swayed as He walked, as though He were carrying a heavy load. His steps were labored as He painfully placed one foot in front of the other. They drew closer to Him, longing to help Him, even though they did not understand His sorrow of spirit.

When they reached the entrance to the garden, most of the disciples stayed, but Jesus chose three to accompany Him further. Then He proceeded to one of His favorite places of prayer, while the disciples who were with Him waited a little distance away. How often we have looked at pictures of this scene— Jesus kneeling, praying in the garden. This was the night when Jesus' soul was exceeding sorrowful, when He felt as if He were going to die.

In considering this experience in Gethsemane, let's follow

through and notice how different ones related to Him—how different ones treated Him in the garden.

First of all, consider His own Father. In the plan that had been laid before the foundation of the world, Jesus and His Father had chosen a course that Jesus was now determined not to deviate from, in spite of the pain. Humanly speaking, He shrank from the terrible ordeal. The time had come when His Father, according to Scripture, had laid on Him the iniquity of us all. It was an overwhelming burden.

There is no way we can understand how heavy a burden it was, but think for a moment concerning some failure in your life, some time in your life when you fell hard, and the enemy came in and beat you over the head with guilt. Can you think of a time in your life when you felt the farthest from God—the most separated—and experienced the weightiest sense of remorse and pain on account of your sin? I have talked with people who felt such a burden in this sinful world, in reaping the results of their own life-style, that they wanted to end it all. Life wasn't worth continuing because of the guilt and pain. All right, take that experience in your life, and then add to it every other time in your life when you experienced guilt or failure or sin. Then multiply that by the number of people in the world, with all of their accumulated guilt. And after you have done that, multiply that heaviness by all the people from every age. This is the guilt that Jesus took upon His shoulders. This is why we cannot even begin to imagine or understand the burden Jesus felt when God laid upon Him the iniquity of us all.

And the amazing thing is that Jesus was just as much involved in this plan as was His Father. God did not place these burdens on Jesus against His will. The Bible tells us that the Father and the Son were together in this reconciliation. And even though God loves the sinner and has always loved sinners, God hates sin. Jesus hated sin. The burden of the sin of the world was crushing out His life, yet Jesus willingly took that burden that God might be just and also the justifier of the one who believes and accepts the sacrifice provided.

In this time of trial in Gethsemane, when Jesus died before He died, there was an apparent separation between Jesus and

His Father. This was the separation the sinner will feel if he persists in rebellion against God and is finally lost forever.

Sometimes we get the idea that when Jesus came to this time, He was dependent upon His own strength. We see that all through His life He had lived in dependence on His Father—in close relationship with His Father. But now, in Gethsemane, and on through to the cross, it looks as if His Father is gone, and Jesus is left to struggle with sin all alone. Right here we need to take a second look—for even though Jesus *felt* forsaken, He was not forsaken. Jesus had predicted His great sorrow in John 16:32, when He said, "Behold, the hour cometh, yea, is now come, that ye shall be scattered, every man to his own, and shall leave me alone: and yet, I am not alone, because the Father is with me." Jesus knew His Father was going to be with Him, but He also knew that He would *feel* absolutely abandoned and separated when the crisis came. The feelings were as real as if He had not known differently. Jesus felt that by sin He was being separated from His Father. He felt that God's wrath against sin was so great that His unity with His Father was destroyed. But God was there. The Father was there, "In Christ, reconciling the world unto himself." See 2 Corinthians 5:19.

Jesus was afraid. He was fearful. He feared He would not be able to go through with this, when He felt separated from His Father. He felt alone. He knew He was human. We could spend a lot of time speculating on the exact details of the human nature of Christ. But we do know this much—He knew by experience the weakness of humanity after 4,000 years of sin. He was not as strong as Adam—and He well knew how Adam had failed the test. He felt alone and forsaken, and it is no wonder He clung to the ground, not wanting to be separated any further than He already felt. No wonder He cried, and sweat and blood came out of His pores. No wonder this death struggle of Jesus in the garden can only be described with words such as *despair* and *horror* and *blackness*. No sorrow can be compared with the sorrow of Jesus. How hard it must have been for Jesus—and also for His Father.

Let's consider someone else at this hour. Going to the other extreme in the picture, let's consider Satan. How was Satan working in this hour of darkness? Satan was coming to his big moment, when everything was at stake. All through Jesus' life Satan had tried to conquer Him—to cause Him to fail. It started way back before His birth. When Jesus was just a baby, all of the boy babies in Bethlehem had lost their lives as Satan made his abortive attempt on the life of Jesus.

Satan had met Jesus in the wilderness and almost succeeded in taking His life, but an angel had come and strengthened Jesus when He was dying in the wilderness of temptation. Satan and his imps had challenged Jesus on more than one occasion, screaming at Him and saying, "We know who you are, the Holy One of God."

Now Satan came to tempt Jesus to think that His Father had left Him for good. Jesus had said, "My Father has not left Me," but Satan said, "Yes, He has! You're all alone. This separation that You're feeling is the real thing. You'll never see Your Father again. The separation You are feeling is eternal, so what point is there in Your going through all of this pain? You're supposed to be saving the world, but the world has rejected You. Even Your own people are interested in destroying You. One of Your disciples has already turned traitor and has betrayed You. Why don't You give up? Why don't you go back to Your Father and stop wasting Your efforts?"

Jesus was tempted to return to His Father. Very interesting. Our big temptation is to live a life apart from God. Jesus' big temptation in the garden was to get back with His Father. Quite the opposite from us, wasn't it? Satan was pulling out all the stops, doing everything he could to convince Jesus to leave the world in his hands. He knew that his own future was teetering in the balance.

Next let's consider the angels. How did the angels react that night as Jesus struggled in the garden? They were silent. Angels knew that the big moment for the universe had come. There was no singing in heaven. No harps were played. The angels were absorbed in watching the drama. They watched— and knew what was involved. And the angels—whose entire lifetime had been filled with the joy of service—were frustrated that night. Can you see them pacing back and forth, looking at the scene, then turning away, wanting to rush on swift wings to bring help, but being unable to do so?

They look at Jesus in the garden. They look at the Father. Oh, if only they could get the nod from the Father to go and help. Finally they have to hide their faces from the awful scene.

More people are involved in the plan of salvation than just those of the earth. There are unfallen worlds. Do you believe that other worlds are inhabited? Have you read Revelation 12 lately? "Rejoice, ye heavens, and ye that dwell in them." Verse 12. A number of clues in the Bible make it quite clear that other worlds are inhabited. I suppose we could speculate about how much of what happens on earth they are able to see. Perhaps they have the same vision the angels have. I doubt that they have television with the six o'clock news and some kind of heavenly Dan Rather. But when the world was created, the morning stars sang together, and all the sons of God shouted for joy. See Job 38:4-7. They were aware of what was going on. And they were also wondering what the outcome would be.

When Satan began his rebellion, he made two charges against God. First, that it is impossible to keep the law of God, and second, that if the law is not kept, forgiveness is impossible. If he was right in his charges, then the whole universe would be in jeopardy. So the unfallen worlds, as well as the angels, were looking on, fascinated and breathless, taking in the scene there in the Garden of Gethsemane.

Next let's consider the disciples. They were sleeping. Have you ever given them bad marks for sleeping? Jesus went to them for sympathy, for Jesus was human, and one of the great principles of the human heart is the longing for sympathy in suffering. It's all right to want comfort when you're hurting. It's legitimate to want to hear someone say, "I'm with you—I'm here."

So Jesus stumbled from His place of retirement and went to the disciples for a word of encouragement. But they were sleeping. They stared at Him for a moment, but could not even rouse themselves sufficiently to give Him any response. Then they slumped back into sleep.

But notice what the Scripture says about what kind of sleep it was. There are different kinds of sleep. There is the sleep of physical exhaustion, when you've walked the dusty roads of Galilee all day long and are tired. There's the sleep of boredom. And there is also the sleep spoken of in Luke 22:45: "When he rose up from prayer, and was come to his disciples, he found them sleeping for sorrow." The sleep of sorrow.

What is the sleep of sorrow? Even psychologists, who study the human mind, tell us about people who use sleep as an escape from some terrible sorrow. Most of us have experienced a bit of it in our lifetimes. The disciples were victims of that kind of sleep. They knew Jesus was suffering. They had heard Him speak of trial and death. They had tried not to hear, but they were afraid. They had heard His groans and cries of agony there in the garden. They were hurting because their beloved Teacher was hurting, and sleep came as a blessed relief from too much pain. The disciples were sleeping the sleep of sorrow.

Jesus knew that, and we ought to remember it, too. Jesus knew their spirits were willing, but that their flesh was weak. In a sense, it wasn't a sleep of forgetting Jesus; it was a sleep of identifying with Him so strongly they could not handle the pressure. That's why they were sleeping.

So the third time Jesus went back, alone, to His place, crying out once more to His Father, "If it be possible, let this cup pass from Me. But if not, Thy will be done."

Nature was the only companion of Jesus in that hour. The olive trees wept as they dropped their dew, the cypress trees bowed in sympathy, and the silence of the night was shattered by the cries of the suffering Saviour. Jesus struggled to the last moment, apparently alone and forsaken by heaven and earth. Don't ever equate Jesus' struggle in the garden with anything we ever go through. We are never in the same category with Jesus as He was on this night. We never will be. We will never be called upon to bear the weight of a whole world's sin. But as Jesus struggled and wept and prayed and finally fell dying, the picture changed.

Gabriel—who took Lucifer's place, who stood in the presence of God—had been pacing back and forth, looking at the Father, looking at the garden. Suddenly, the Father gives Gabriel the nod! And Gabriel leaves at supernatural speed—the speed of the universe—for a flight of 105 trillion miles or more, which he will make in less than three minutes! I can hear all the hosts of angels shouting, "*Go*, Gabriel!"

Gabriel goes. He arrives at the side of Jesus. He lifts Jesus' head from the dirt. He holds Jesus' head against his shoulder. And he points to the open heavens from whence he has come. He has come to remind Jesus of His Father's love. He tells Him of the souls who will be saved eternally as a result of His sacrifice. He assures Him that the Father is greater and more powerful than Satan and that the kingdoms of this world will be won for the saints of the Most High. He tells Him that this awful sacrifice will be worth it, worth it forever, because of those from our race who will be with Him in heaven throughout eternity.

And Jesus stands up from His place of prayer. He holds His head high and walks out of the garden to meet the mob. He holds His head high, like the King He is, from that moment straight through to the cross. As they push and shove Him all the way to Calvary, He has a strength and a composure that is supernatural. He has accepted His Father's love and power by faith alone. Even though He *feels* alone on the cross and cries out, "Why have You forsaken Me?" He is not alone. At the very end He says, "Father, into Thy hands I commit My spirit." See Luke 23:46.

Are you glad for the story of Jesus? Are you glad for what He went through? Are you glad that you can be one of those who are eternally saved because of Him? Why not thank Him again today for His amazing love?

How Peter Treated Jesus

To spank, or not to spank, is a question that all parents face. Studies have shown that the kind of discipline is not nearly so important as that a child know he's loved and accepted along with the discipline. But my father chose to spank!

When we were small, he used something light. One day, after I had experienced a spanking, I came to my mother with a smile on my face and said, "That didn't even hurt!" That was one of my biggest mistakes. Because she told my father what I had said, and he made sure from then on to do it right! But the worst spanking I ever got was the time when my father didn't even touch me.

We were on vacation on an island in the middle of Gull Lake in Michigan. My brother and I were at it again, fighting. That was our favorite pastime. We were spoiling the vacation for ourselves and particularly for our parents. My father tried everything he could think of to get us to stop. He tried taking away our dessert. He tried sending us to bed without supper. He tried making us stay in the cabin. He tried spanking. Nothing worked. Finally the moment came when he called us in before him again, there in the cabin, and he was trying to think of some other way to go. But he was obviously at the end of his ideas. And then I saw the tears begin to come. Seeing tears on the face of my big, strong father was something new to me. I realized I had caused disappointment and heartache to one who loved me, and I couldn't stand the tears. I could take any kind of punishment but that. Suddenly, I really wanted to change. It was the worst licking I ever got!

This was a lesson Peter learned. We left off in the last chapter in Matthew 26—the experience of Jesus in the Garden of Gethsemane. The angel had returned to heaven, and Jesus is telling His disciples to go ahead and sleep now. "And while he yet spake, lo, Judas, one of the twelve, came, and with him a great multitude with swords and staves, from the chief priests and elders of the people." Verse 47. "In that same hour said Jesus to the multitudes, Are you come out as against a thief with swords and staves for to take me? I sat daily with you teaching in the temple, and ye laid no hold on me. But all this was done, that the scriptures of the prophets might be fulfilled. Then all the disciples forsook him, and fled." Verses 55, 56.

The disciples had been suddenly awakened, there in the garden. Judas had led the mob to Jesus, giving the kiss that was a sign that this was the One. Peter had taken up his sword and amputated the ear of the high priest's servant. As Jesus spoke briefly with them, an angel stepped between Jesus and the mob, and for a moment it looked as if their plans were defeated. But the angel departed again, and the disciples, who had vowed that they would never forsake Jesus, fled into the darkness. Even Peter—who had been the most vehement, saying, "The rest of them may leave, but I won't,"—even Peter forsook Him and fled.

And then the mob took Jesus to the palace of Caiaphas. There they tried to find false witnesses who would come up with the kind of charge that would make Jesus worthy of death. But the false witnesses conflicted—and their testimony did not agree. Jesus waited patiently, not speaking a word, until at last Caiaphas was desperate. He commanded Jesus, under oath, to tell whether or not He was the Christ, the Son of God.

At that point Jesus did not remain silent. He said, "I am." And as every ear listened to His admission under oath before the high priest and every eye beheld, the face of Jesus shone with a heavenly light. Then Jesus added something Caiaphas hadn't asked for. He said, "Hereafter shall ye see the Son of man sitting on the right hand of power, and coming in the clouds of heaven." Verse 64.

Caiaphas shouted, "Blasphemy!" And the mob, aroused, began to push and shove and spit upon Him. It was awful that night in Caiaphas's judgment hall. They put an old rag over His head and struck Him and asked, "If You're a prophet, why don't You tell who hit You?" They spit in His face. And Jesus was treated as cruelly and unfairly as ever a prisoner was treated.

But a deeper anguish came to Jesus that night. It's this deeper anguish we need to consider, for it involved one of His closest followers.

The disciples had taken off on a hundred-yard dash through the garden when the mob had taken Jesus, but at least two of them had turned around and followed at a distance as the crowd made their way back to the hall of Caiaphas. They were Peter and John. They couldn't stay away for very long.

When they entered the hall, John found a place as near to Jesus as he possibly could, but Peter joined the crowd by the fire, warming himself in the cool night air and trying to pretend. It's a familiar story. But sometimes we don't stop to consider carefully the steps Peter had taken to bring himself to the place where he could deny his Lord.

The first step came when Jesus tried to warn Peter of His danger. Jesus had said, "All ye shall be offended because of me this night: for it is written, I will smite the shepherd, and the sheep of the flock shall be scattered abroad."

But Peter answered, "Though all men shall be offended because of thee, yet will I never be offended."

Jesus said, "This night, before the cock crow, thou shalt deny me thrice."

Peter insisted, "Though I should die with thee, yet will I not deny thee." Matthew 26:31-34. He was sure of himself. He felt strong. He was sure he had enough willpower and backbone to make the right decision and follow through with it. He considered himself a self-disciplined man—one whom Jesus could count on. He did not realize his danger. That's the first step anyone takes in denying his Lord.

His second step toward the denial was to give in to the temptation to sleep when he should have been praying. It's an easy step to take when you are feeling self-sufficient. Who needs to pray when you can do it yourself? Who needs a higher power if you have plenty of power and strength yourself? I'd like to propose that one of the main reasons the majority of Christians do not spend much time in prayer is that they do not feel the need of help from God that often. They're doing all right by themselves. They find it easy to turn over for an extra hour of sleep in the morning rather than spending time in communion with Christ, for they don't feel the need of prayer that much. And that leads to the next step.

The third step Peter took was to begin to fight his own battles. He thought he was big enough to take on the enemy in his own strength. He tackled the whole mob with his one sword. But all he got was one ear—and it wasn't even a particularly important ear, except to the high priest's servant to whom it belonged!

When we have separated ourselves from the source of strength, we forget that we are never to fight the enemy ourselves. We forget that God is the only one who can fight our battles for us. He's the only one strong enough. And when we begin swinging our swords, the inevitable result is defeat and shame.

The fourth step Peter took that night was to try to save himself. Jesus didn't join in with him and help him fight his own battles in the way Peter expected. So he started running. If Jesus wasn't big enough to save him, then he'd better save himself. And Peter took off into the darkness.

The fifth step Peter took was to follow Jesus afar off. His trust in Jesus had taken a beating. He wasn't ready to completely and permanently cut himself off from Christ, but he was being careful now. He didn't want to get too close. He deliberately kept some distance between himself and Jesus. And so he followed Jesus from afar.

But the night was cold. The night is always cold when we find ourselves far away from Jesus. Have you discovered that yet? So Peter took the sixth step of seeking warmth and comfort where the world finds warmth and comfort. He joined the rest of the mob by the fire, trying to warm himself there. But he found himself strangely uncomfortable in that setting, which led him to take the next step, the seventh, of assuming a false identity. He wasn't fitting in too well. When the rest of the rabble would laugh as Jesus was mistreated, Peter found himself wanting to cry. But that would draw attention to him, and they'd notice that he wasn't really one of them. So he forced himself to laugh louder than any of them. When the rest of the crowd would curse and jest, it jarred on Peter's spirit. He was playing a part and not doing too well, because it wasn't long before he was noticed.

And that's when he found himself at the final step of denying Jesus altogether. When a person has separated from Jesus and is finding his warmth and acceptance in the world and someone says, "Aren't you one of them?" he says, "No, I'm not!" That's the way it goes. When the heat was on and they were pointing the finger at Peter, he took the final step as he began to curse and swear and to deny with an oath that he ever had known Jesus.

Right at that moment, Jesus turned and looked at Peter. Jesus turned from where He was being shoved and pushed and crowded. Jesus—wearing the crown of thorns and with blood dripping quietly down—turned and looked at Peter. There are different kinds of looks. When Jesus looked at Peter, it wasn't a look of anger or disgust. It was a look of pity and love for His poor disciple.

We probably wouldn't claim Peter as a disciple of Jesus right then. Even Peter was denying it. But Jesus saw that Peter was still His. Peter wasn't a hypocrite. He had really meant it when he said he would die for Jesus. But Peter was weak. And Peter had been led away, step by step, from the side of Jesus, from trusting fully in Him. Peter hadn't even noticed the process until now. The devil always works this way. He doesn't take us in one gigantic leap off the cliff. He knows we'd see our danger and call upon Jesus immediately. So he takes us from here, to here, to here, in little tiny steps that are as innocent-looking as possible, so we won't realize our need.

Jesus looked on Peter with love and disappointment and sorrow. If Jesus ever needed a friend, it was then. If He ever needed someone to let Him know they were still with Him, still on His side, it was then. That is why the greatest anguish to the heart of Jesus came that night, when one of His closest friends denied even knowing Him.

As Peter's gaze met that of Jesus, a flood of memories swept over him. He remembered the call by the sea, when Jesus had said, I will make you fishers of men. He remembered the night on the lake when he had almost drowned because of his presumption, but Jesus had reached out His hand and saved him. He remembered how Jesus had come to his rescue in the hassle over the temple tax. He remembered how just a few hours before, Jesus had washed his feet, patiently explaining away his protests. He remembered how Jesus had said to him, "Peter, Satan has desired to have you, that he might sift you as wheat. But I have prayed for you. I have prayed for you. I have prayed for you—" See Luke 22:31, 32.

And as Peter saw the pale, suffering face of Jesus, the quivering lips, the drops of blood, he couldn't stand it. He broke from the scene and ran out of the courtyard and down the streets of the darkened city of Jerusalem. He came to the golden gate and ran down the hill and across the brook Kedron. He ran up the other side to the Garden of Gethsemane and groped around until he found the spot where Jesus had prayed and cried and sweat blood drops that night. And Peter fell on his face and wished he could die. He knew that of all the pain Jesus had borne that night, what he had done had cut the deepest. And that knowledge cut Peter to the very heart.

Peter was never the same again after that night in the garden. The crisis of his life had passed. The love and forgiveness of Jesus gave him hope, and ever afterward he was able to speak with assurance and certainty of the good news of what Jesus was willing to do for even the weakest of His children.

Another that night also wished he could die, and he was able to succeed in the attempt. His name was Judas. Judas was probably the smartest of the twelve disciples. He had understood the teaching of Jesus about the kind of kingdom He planned to set up, and he walked away from it after one final, desperate attempt to force Jesus into his way of working. At the feeding of the multitude, Judas had tried to force Jesus to set up

His kingdom with earthly power. Now he tried again to force Jesus to the throne. Have you ever *fought* to put Jesus on the throne in your life?

Judas had hatched a master plot. It really went much farther than the thirty pieces of silver he received from the Jewish leaders. His real purpose was to force Jesus to set up an earthly kingdom—to put Himself on the throne. He thought that if he betrayed Jesus into the hands of the religious leaders, He would be forced to work a miracle to save Himself, and thereby the kingdom of Jesus as the new Messiah would be established. Judas was certain that out of respect for his clever methods, Jesus would appoint him prime minister.

All went well until the time in the garden when Judas betrayed the Lord with a kiss. Then he said to the priests and rulers, "Hold Him fast." He fully expected that Jesus would force His enemies to their knees, free Himself and His disciples, and take over the throne of Israel.

But instead, Judas watched from a distance as Jesus was led as a lamb to the slaughter. He saw the hands of Jesus bound. He saw Him abused in the mockery of a trial before Caiaphas. And as the trial drew to a close, a dread began to sweep over him that he had sold Jesus to His death.

Then came one of the most dramatic moments in the trial of Jesus. Judas couldn't stand it any longer. The scene is described in the book *The Desire of Ages*: "Suddenly a hoarse voice rang through the hall, sending a thrill of terror to all hearts: He is innocent; spare Him, O Caiaphas!

"The tall form of Judas was now seen pressing through the startled throng. His face was pale and haggard, and great drops of sweat stood on his forehead. Rushing to the throne of judgment, he threw down before the high priest the pieces of silver that had been the price of his Lord's betrayal. Eagerly grasping the robe of Caiaphas, he implored him to release Jesus, declaring that He had done nothing worthy of death.

" 'I have sinned,' again cried Judas, 'in that I have betrayed innocent blood.' "—Pages 721, 722.

Then he cast himself at Jesus' feet and pled with Jesus to save Himself. But all that Jesus replied was, "For this hour I have come into the world."

Well, you know the rest of the story of Judas. Later, on the way to Calvary, the jostling throng were stopped in their tracks at the foot of a tree where lay the broken body of Judas, now severed from the rope he had used to hang himself.

The trial before Caiaphas closed quickly after the confession of Judas before the assembly. His admission of guilt in betraying Jesus had put the high priest in an uncomfortable light, and Caiaphas was eager to escape the questioning looks and embarrassment.

It was early morning now, and whatever they could hope to accomplish must be done quickly. It was Friday—the beginning of the Passover—and the mob spirit which had carried things along this far was already beginning to wane. If they were forced to wait until after the Sabbath, they could have little hope of pushing through to their goal.

So the trial of Jesus before the highest religious leaders of God's chosen nation was brought to a close. These priests and ministers of His own temple had examined Him and condemned Him. They now declared Him worthy of death. Wonder, O heavens, and be astonished O earth!

How They Treated Jesus in Pilate's Judgment Hall

"Then led they Jesus from Caiaphas unto the hall of judgment: and it was early; and they themselves went not into the judgment hall, lest they should be defiled; but that they might eat the passover." John 18:28.

What a scene for the universe to witness! The Judge of all the earth was brought to trial. He was the One who had created heaven and earth. He had created the ones who pushed and shoved Him all the way to the judgment hall of Pilate. He was keeping their hearts beating in their chests even as they accused Him. And He stood there silently, fully realizing that the day would come when those very people would stand before Him and hear His sentence pronounced on them for time and eternity, when He would be the Judge of all.

Have you ever worried about the day of judgment? Have you ever been afraid and perhaps tried not to think about it, because the very thought made you uneasy? Just remember three things as you look forward to the coming judgment.

First, remember that you will be judged fairly. When Jesus was brought to judgment, He had to face the experience knowing that He would *not* be judged fairly. He knew that those who accused Him were looking for any excuse to condemn Him. Even more than that, not finding any valid excuse to condemn Him, they would condemn Him anyway on false charges. The court before which He stood was corrupt and rotten to the core. In spite of the fact that all they really had against Him was that His sinless life was a reproach to those who were so sinful, not one voice was raised in His defense. He didn't have a ghost of a chance of being found innocent, according to their standard of judgment.

When you are brought to judgment, you will be judged fairly. Is that good news or bad news? Are you innocent or guilty? Are you a sinner or not? If you are brought to a fair and just court, to be judged as to whether or not you have been a sinner, what will the decision be? No wonder we often look forward to the day of judgment with apprehension and concern. We know that if we are judged fairly, we will be condemned! We will be found guilty. We don't have a ghost of a chance of being found innocent, when measured by the law of God, His standard in the judgment.

But don't stop yet! There is a second thing to remember in considering the judgment. When Jesus was brought to trial, He stood alone. There was no one on His side. No one was defending Him against the charges brought against Him. The prosecution was there in full force—but the defense was strangely absent.

There will be a prosecution, in the day when we stand before the judgment bar of God. But we will also have a Defender, an Advocate with the Father, Jesus Christ the righteous. We won't have to stand alone before the accusations of the enemy. There will be One who will stand by our side. And He has not only been tempted as we have been tempted, He has also been brought to trial. He has also been condemned. And He has paid the penalty that He didn't deserve, that He might now place His own righteousness to our account so that we might be acquitted, which was what He deserved. He stood trial *for* us. He was condemned *for* us. He was punished *for* us.

And of course, the final thing we need to remember when we think of the coming day of judgment is that this same Jesus who is our Defender and who has stood trial for us and has taken our punishment for us, is going to be our Judge as well. What more could He do to insure that we will be given every opportunity for pardon?

But for Him, on that day before Pilate, there was no hope of pardon, no mercy, no justice. The Jewish leaders who dragged Him before Pilate wouldn't even come into the judgment hall. They wanted to be ceremonially clean for the coming Passover, which pointed to His death for them. So they insisted that He be condemned to death from the outer court so they could be home in time for the beginning of the Passover weekend. Sin does strange things to our human judgment, doesn't it?

"Pilate then went out unto them, and said, What accusation bring ye against this man? They answered and said unto him, If he were not a malefactor, we would not have delivered him up unto thee." In other words, Don't question us! We are the ones in charge here. We are the leaders of this nation. Don't you know who you are talking to?

"Then said Pilate unto them, Take ye him, and judge him according to your law." He said, If you're in charge, then why are you bringing Him to me? "The Jews therefore said unto him, It is not lawful for us to put any man to death: that the saying of Jesus might be fulfilled, which he spake, signifying what death he should die. Then Pilate entered into the judgment hall again, and called Jesus, and said unto him, Art thou the King of the Jews? Jesus answered him, Sayest thou this thing of thyself, or did others tell it thee of me? Pilate answered, Am I a Jew? Thine own nation and the chief priests have delivered thee unto me: what hast thou done? Jesus answered, My kingdom is not of this world: if my kingdom were of this world, then would my servants fight, that I should not be delivered to the Jews: but now is my kingdom not from hence." John 18:29-36.

Notice particularly the phrase, "My kingdom is not of this world: if my kingdom were of this world, then would my servants fight." Judas had been determined to force Jesus to the throne—to fight to put Him there. That was his style. He believed in fighting for what he wanted. He believed in putting forth effort, in trying to make things happen for himself. He didn't believe in waiting for God to work. He wanted to do it himself.

But Jesus says, "My kingdom is not of this world. If it were, *then* would my servants fight." Because His kindgom wasn't of

this world, then His servants were not supposed to fight to accomplish their goals. Could it be that we are not supposed to
fight to bring victory in the spiritual kingdom as well?

If you trace the usage of the word *kingdom* in the Gospels,
you discover that Jesus is speaking of either the kingdom of
grace—or the kingdom of glory. He used the term *kingdom*, or
kingdom of heaven, repeatedly. Often His parables began with
the words, "The kingdom of heaven is like unto—"

The kingdom of grace includes both God's forgiveness and
His power. And for neither of these gifts are the servants of God
supposed to fight. We cannot earn or merit our way to heaven.
Nor can we fight to obtain victory and obedience and overcoming. If Jesus' kingdom were of this world, then His servants
would need to fight sin and the devil, fight to obey, fight to surrender, fight for victory. But Jesus said, "My kingdom is not of
this world."

The blessings of the heavenly kingdom are to be received as
gifts. Forgiveness is a gift. Repentance is a gift. Victory is a
gift. Obedience is a gift. And you don't fight for what is given to
you as a gift.

Peter had misunderstood. He had swung his sword and then
run away from Jesus when he saw that fighting was not where
it was at. Now he was facedown in the garden, wishing he could
die. Judas had misunderstood. Now he lay in a lifeless heap
under the branch of a tree along the road to Calvary. Pilate
misunderstood and chose to give attention to the clamor of the
mob rather than to the quiet words of Jesus, who offered him
the gift of a kingdom where fighting would not be necessary.
Then he tried to evade the painful decision by sending Jesus to
Herod, who had also misunderstood the nature of Christ's kingdom. Pilate decided to pass the buck to Herod.

"When Herod saw Jesus, he was exceeding glad: for he was
desirous to see him of a long season, because he had heard
many things of him; and he hoped to have seen some miracle
done by him. Then he questioned with him in many words; but
he answered him nothing." Jesus did not speak a single word to
Herod. "And the chief priests and scribes stood and vehemently
accused him. And Herod with his men of war set him at nought,

and mocked him, and arrayed him in a gorgeous robe, and sent him again to Pilate." Luke 23:8-11.

When I first read this story, I was happy. Herod was the one who had killed John the Baptist—the one who, at his drunken party, had made the rash oath to Salome. So for a long time it seemed even *Christian* to rejoice in seeing the cold treatment Herod got from Jesus that day! That was my reaction. That's the way to treat Herod, Lord! Good for Herod! Ignore him. Snub him. Be vindictive. I was glad to realize that to be thus ignored would have been the hardest blow Herod could have received.

But then I came to understand that Jesus is not that way. Jesus came to die for Herod, as well as for you and me. So you don't see Jesus standing there with His chin out, getting even. Instead, you see Jesus with His chin quivering, with silent tears flowing, because another one of His beautiful created friends has turned Him down. You see Jesus with breaking heart accepting the decision that Herod had already made.

How did Herod come to make this decision against Christ? By rejecting the spirit of prophecy! (How do you like that? You didn't expect that to show up here, did you? But it's true!) John the Baptist was one of the greatest prophets. In fact, according to the Gospel record, John the Baptist was more than a prophet. He was called the Lord's messenger. And the tragic conclusion of the story of Herod is that if you are unfriendly to the Lord's messenger, unfriendly to the prophets, you're going to be unfriendly to Jesus as well. The two always go together.

"If they hear not Moses and the prophets, neither will they be persuaded, though one rose from the dead." Luke 16:31. Herod had rejected the truth spoken to him by the prophet, and no other message was to be given to him. Jesus accepted Herod's choice, because there was no other way to reach his heart.

In anger and humiliation, Herod sent Jesus back again to the court of Pilate. Let's pick up the story in Matthew 27. This time we have Mrs. Pilate coming into the picture. "When he was set down on the judgment seat, his wife sent unto him, saying, Have thou nothing to do with that just man: for I have suffered many things this day in a dream because of him." Matthew 27:19.

Perhaps it had been weeks or even months earlier. Pilate and Mrs. Pilate were sitting down at the breakfast table. Pilate was eating his rolls and drinking his coffee, and Mrs. Pilate was helping him to the morning paper, the Jerusalem *Times*! She called his attention to the headlines and the notices here and there that had to do with Jesus from Nazareth. She must have heard of Jesus and had a soft spot in her heart for Him before this time. She must have been seeking for truth.

She was the kind of person God could communicate with, and she had a dream which caused her suffering. She saw Jesus on trial in the judgment hall. She saw that her husband did not release Him as he should have done. She saw the cross of Calvary and the bleeding body of Jesus stretched between heaven and earth. She heard His cry, "It is finished." Then she saw even further into the future, to the time when Jesus returns to the earth in power and majesty. It was then that she awoke and sent the urgent message to her husband, warning Him from the mistake he was about to make.

But still Pilate went straight ahead, unwillingly, wishing for some way both to release Jesus and pacify the angry crowd. But in the end, he caved in and sacrificed Jesus to try to keep the approval of the multitude. Which takes us back to John 18 again. Pilate is trying one last desperate trick with the mob and its leaders. He says, "Ye have a custom, that I should release unto you one at the passover: will ye therefore that I release unto you the King of the Jews? Then cried they all again, saying, Not this man, but Barabbas. Now Barabbas was a robber." John 18:39, 40.

Fulton Oursler, in his book *The Greatest Story Ever Told*, depicts Barabbas as a zealot—a dagger man against Rome. He was well known as a thief and robber. But the religious leaders chose Barabbas, which was in essence choosing lawlessness. In choosing Barabbas, they were choosing one who did not believe that the law must be obeyed. If they had chosen Jesus, they would have chosen respect for God's law, for obedience and overcoming.

How subtle that the same issues have arisen even within the church today. Once again we find the choice between Christ and Barabbas. Which are you choosing in your life? Are you accepting fellowship and communion with Christ as a way of life, as the method for receiving His gifts of forgiveness and victory? Or are you choosing Barabbas, fighting your own battles and settling for a belief that the law does not need to be obeyed?

The people of Israel had made their choice. They chose Barabbas. The decision was never reversed.

"Then the soldiers of the governor took Jesus into the common hall, and gathered unto him the whole band of soldiers. And they stripped him, and put on him a scarlet robe. And when they had platted a crown of thorns, they put it upon his head, and a reed in his right hand: and they bowed the knee before him, and mocked him, saying, Hail, King of the Jews! And they spit upon him, and took the reed, and smote him on the head. And after that they had mocked him, they took the robe off from him, and put his own raiment on him, and led him away to crucify him." Matthew 27:27-31.

And Jesus, who as Creator of the universe could have in a moment summoned the assistance of ten thousand angels to release Him from the awful scene, continued to submit to death, for your sake and mine—even the death of the cross.

The Way of the Cross

Pretend you are Simon.

You have come on a long journey to reach Palestine. Your home is in North Africa, but you and your wife and two sons, Alexander and Rufus, now live somewhere near Jerusalem. On this particular morning you are coming in from the country early in the morning. That's rather unusual. As you know, people in this part of the country work outside the city walls by day, tilling the soil, and return at night to the safety of the city. Perhaps on this particular day you have forgotten your hoe or some other tool needed for your work. But you enter the city just at the right time to meet a strange procession.

You see soldiers trying to control the mob, priests and rulers in their long robes, and people of all rank and file. They are following three men who carry crosses. You see nine men following at a distance, with shame and sorrow on their faces.

You look more closely at the three men who are obviously condemned. Two of them are thieves. They are well-built, muscular, hard-faced, and struggling with the soldiers who are forcing them along. They are well able to carry the burden forced on their shoulders.

The third Man is also strong, well-built, and muscular. He has worked in a carpenter shop, without benefit of power tools, for most of His life. But there's something different about Him. There's an expression on His face that catches your attention. He is bruised and battered. He has been through something the other two have not. Since the day before, He has been without

food and drink. He has struggled alone in the Garden of Gethsemane, in conflict with the powers of darkness. He has stood
trial no less than seven times. He has been abused by the mob.
He has twice been scourged. And now His human nature can
bear no more. As you watch, He falls fainting beneath the cross.

Of the nine men who are His followers—surely one of them
will step forward in this crucial time. Three of the original
twelve are missing. One lies mangled and dead at the foot of a
tree a little further up the pathway. Another is still facedown
in the garden called Gethsemane, with a breaking heart for
having denied his Best Friend. And a third will show up a little
later, much to our surprise and joy.

But these nine men are holding back. They are filled with
grief, bowed down with disappointed hopes. They keep their
distance. They are filled with sorrow over the pain of their Master, yet they stay away, giving in to fear and shame. Not one of
them is willing to offer Him assistance.

And you, Simon, are amazed and dismayed. You are not the
retiring type. You don't keep things bottled up inside of you. So
you exclaim, "This is incredible! Why doesn't someone help this
Man?"

The soldiers hear you. They have been at a loss to know what
to do. It is apparent to all who watch that it is impossible for
Jesus to bear the cross any farther. He can scarcely stand—
even without the load of heavy timbers. So the soldiers gladly
seize this opportunity to take you by force and place the cross of
this third man on your shoulders.

Perhaps your first response is to think, "Well, that's what I
get for opening my mouth." But as you take the cross and join
the procession, you hear the name of this One for whom your
sympathy was aroused. It is Jesus. Jesus! Your two sons,
Alexander and Rufus, have told you about this Man. They have
seen Him before. They have heard His teaching. They came
home, excitement on their faces, telling you that they believed
Him to be the Messiah. You had always intended to investigate
further, but had never taken the time to follow through. Now
you are being forced to carry His cross.

Right here, I would like to pause for a moment in this story. I would like to invite you who read to consider—have you ever been forced to carry the cross? Are you a second- or third- or fourth-generation church member, whose parents and grandparents have forced you to carry His cross? Are you a young person from a Christian home, forced to carry His cross? Are you employed within the church as a teacher, minister, or some other church employee, and you feel that in order to keep your job you are forced to carry His cross? I would like to remind you that that's not all bad. Please watch for the blessing of Simon as we continue the story.

You continue to carry the cross up the road toward Calvary, and you begin to look around you at the people in the crowd. The priests and rulers have joined in with the lowest of society, throwing insults and mockery in the face of Jesus. They are hooting and howling with the rest of the mob. The soldiers with their whips and swords continue trying to keep the procession on the road, although you notice that frequently one of them will turn toward Jesus with a lingering glance.

The mob is made up largely of those who love excitement, no matter what the source. They are people who can join the triumphal procession one day, and shout, "Hosannah to the King"—and then join in crying, "Crucify Him"—just because it's the popular thing to do. They are the ones who follow wherever the crowd goes in its ebb and flow. They don't think for themselves but follow voices, joining in with the voices that shout the loudest at any given moment.

Some in this crowd have been healed by Jesus, which proves that it takes something more than a mere miracle to make you a believer. Some have taken their loved ones to Jesus and received the help that He never refused to give. But now they are just part of the mob, indistinguishable among the throng.

The procession pauses. Nearby is a group of women—women who possess sensitive natures. Women whose tears flow easily when confronted by sorrow and pain. These women are the only ones Jesus seems to notice. And He stops to speak to them.

We would like to think that these women were true believers in Jesus, that they accepted Him as the Messiah and were weeping for Him as their Lord and Saviour. But the evidence is that they were weeping simply from the drama and emotion of the moment. It is possible to weep today if the right button in the nervous system is pushed. Tears can flow and then cease to flow, and the person remains unchanged. Perhaps that's why Jesus said to them, "Don't weep for me, but weep for yourselves and for your children." He tries to point them beyond the emotion of the moment to the real need of their hearts.

Suddenly you spot the third of the missing disciples. It's John—the disciple who has always been there with Jesus. He had not abandoned Jesus in this time of crisis. He is supporting Mary, the mother of Jesus, in her hour of need. Surely John would have carried the cross of Jesus if he had not already undertaken this important task. Now he walks with Mary as she follows as close to her Son as she can.

You watch Mary for a few moments. Her face is covered with tears. She leans on John for support, but follows determinedly in the footsteps of her beloved Son. Perhaps she is remembering the day the angel came, telling her of the Son soon to be born to her. Perhaps she is picturing a little eight-year-old boy taking the scroll under His arm and heading out to the hills in the early morning for an uninterrupted time of communion with His heavenly Father. Perhaps she recalls the day He closed up the carpenter shop, kissed her good-bye, and left on His strange mission. And perhaps she is remembering, with sinking heart, His words predicting this very event. She may have heard again the words of Simeon in the temple, "This child is set for the fall and rising of many in Israel, and the sword shall pierce through thine own soul." See Luke 2:34, 35. Even now the sword is cutting and hurting.

But all along the way to the cross, the One you watch most earnestly is the One whose cross you are carrying. Your heart is torn as you see the intense agony He suffers. You see His stumbling step, His bent form, His blood drops endlessly falling. You see the look of peace and acceptance, even amid the pain. You see His willingness to struggle along the road to Calvary.

The thieves fight and try to escape. The soldiers must constantly watch to keep them in line. But this One whose cross you bear is different. He goes willingly, even though He can scarcely put one foot in front of the other. And you watch and you wonder, until finally the destination has been reached.

The thieves are overpowered by the Roman soldiers and placed on their crosses. But Jesus meekly submits, lying down and stretching out His hands while they bring the hammers and nails. You hear the sobs of Jesus' mother, the curses of the thieves and soldiers, the insults of the mob. And then you hear Jesus' own voice, and you bend to catch His words. You hear Him say, "Father, forgive them, for they know not what they do."

Suddenly your heart is broken with love for this Man. And you cry out, Father, forgive me too. Forgive me for waiting. Forgive me for putting off the decision to find out more about this Man. Forgive me for doubting when my sons told me about Jesus. And forgive me for resenting having to carry His cross.

And as you look down at Him through your tears, He says to you, "Thank you, Simon. Thank you for carrying My cross."

And as you look back at Him, you say, "Thank You. Thank You, Lord."

You have seen a little of how Jesus treated people. You have seen how people treated Jesus in return. There are only two choices in the end. You can join the soldiers in nailing Jesus to the cross, crucifying Him afresh. Or you can join Simon in carrying His cross. Only two choices—and the choice is up to you.